Praise for **differentiated**

Differentiated presents the most exciting and compelling strategic approach I've encountered in years. One of the book's greatest strengths is the unique right-brain and left-brain approach that springs from the author's work as a strategist and an artist. Reading this book brings joy and hope. Karla shows you how to have an artist's eye and apply a master strategist's tools to succeed at discovering your zone.
Rebecca Chopp | Chancellor Emerita, University of Denver

Karla has created a fresh strategic framework that today's organizations absolutely need. Witnessing this framework in action is a magical experience, and nothing comes close to aligning stakeholders quicker. It's an essential tool that leads to meaningful conversations and positive strategic outcomes. I highly recommend it!
Naveed Usman | CEO, The Usman Group

Differentiated is inspirational. Take the time right now and read this book. It contains so much original thinking. It challenges you to consider who you are serving and whether you truly understand what matters most to them. Differentiated reminds me a bit of Good to Great. *A terrific storyteller, Karla's real-world examples keep you engaged and bring actionable insights to life.*
James Holmes | Executive Director, Cherokee Ranch & Castle Foundation

This is a powerful call to action. Karla has created a process that honors who we are and positions us to stand out from the competition. Congratulations on what is clearly a new way forward. We're honored to be a part of your discovery.
Markus Hunt | Head of School, The Logan School for Creative Learning

differentiated

THE BREAKTHROUGH APPROACH TO STRATEGY FOR ORGANIZATIONS DRIVEN BY PURPOSE

Karla Raines

2021

Differentiated: The Breakthrough Approach to Strategy for Organizations Driven by Purpose

By Karla Raines

Differentiation Zone is a trademark of Corona Research, Inc. Reg. No. 6,004,143

Published by My Life is a Work of Art Press, an imprint of Corona Research, Inc.

Copyright © 2021 Karla Raines

ISBN Hardcover Color Print Book: 978-1-7364770-0-7
ISBN Paperback Color Print Book: 978-1-7364770-1-4
ISBN eBook: 978-1-7364770-2-1

13 12 11 10 9 8 7 6 5 4 3 2 1

Contents

Foreword

I have led countless strategy processes throughout my career. Karla Raines's *Differentiated* presents the most exciting and compelling strategic approach I've encountered in years. One of the book's greatest strengths is the unique right-brain and left-brain approach that springs from the author's work as a strategist and an artist.

Differentiated reminds us of our commitment to deliver mission impact for those we are dedicated to serving. It's easy to become distracted by stakeholders' competing voices, each clamoring to matter the most. This is a dilemma that leads to what Karla calls the Zone of Indifference—a place where we focus on meeting the needs of stakeholders instead of the customer, protecting some tradition instead of creating a new future.

The tired ways aren't going to take us into the future we must create. I share Karla's declaration—it's time to say goodbye to SWOT analysis. We must retire the old methods of planning where one size fits all and competitors (or those we emulate) define our strategic direction.

Our organizations must refine and focus on our differentiation. To do this, we must understand our customers, who want to know how we uniquely add value to their lives. If we can't answer this question, they don't care if our methods are as good as or better than our competitors.

Like many, I first bristled at the term "customer" because it sounded transactional or commercial. But this book convinced me to work through my resistance and, in doing so, realize what matters most when planning for our future. Karla teaches us that without a laser-focus on the customers and clarity about what they want and need, we cannot deliver mission impact.

This book is full of valuable learning moments and concepts that challenge outdated thinking. Each chapter opens with a real-world story that illustrates the practices to follow. Karla's examples allow us to see differentiation in action, how to set ourselves apart by questioning our assumptions, and how to transform guesswork into grounded decision-making.

Reading this book brings joy and hope. Now, more than ever, we must create a relevant future for our organizations. Karla shows you how to have an artist's eye and apply a master strategist's tools to succeed at discovering your zone.

Rebecca Chopp
Chancellor Emerita
University of Denver

Introduction

I walked to the front of the lunchroom at The Logan School for Creative Learning and took my place next to the projector's image. I could see the skepticism and hopefulness, too, on those seventy-five faces. Some stood with crossed arms; others sat in kid-sized chairs, with elbows on their knees, listening with intention. The teachers and staff were as ready as they were going to be, justifiably worried that we'd done nothing more than write a bit of lingo to sell the school. My colleague teed me up with a powerful data story. His ability to bring data to life with a caring voice and smart delivery wowed the group. The research made sense. The trust level was increasing. Perhaps the reluctance was falling away, and the school could embrace our discovery. Logan's differentiators were up next.

By then, I'd absorbed it all—the school tours, meetings with the board, stakeholder interviews, parent focus groups, visioning exercises, and EXPO. Those myriad experiences brought together head and heart, the intellectual and the emotional. I'd intuited their feelings, heard their stories, witnessed their mission in action, and read the research reports. I trusted my iterative process to surface early ideas and potential insights and then test and reassess as additional information emerged until the insights were inescapable. Ongoing dialogue with my colleagues reinforced the essential truths.

This time the experience was groundbreaking. Crucial realizations coalesced in an unforeseen way as we compared Logan with the promises, features, and attributes of fourteen competitors.

+ We understood what mattered most to gifted students.
+ We affirmed Logan's unique attributes.

That nexus, like the marker on a map, signified the destination—a unique intersection that only Logan could claim. The Logan model had proven that these kids were capable of driving their education from a young age. Creative thinking affirmed the realization. Logan was clearly differentiated.

We discovered Logan's Differentiation Zone®.

Let's return to the lunchroom for a minute. The mood and energy shifted as we concluded our remarks. Suspicion was replaced by smiles as the entire lunchroom erupted in applause. Logan's differentiators felt as authentic and powerful to the school community as they did to us. The school's uniqueness had been proudly affirmed. We honored what mattered most to the gifted kids who matter most to Logan.

This life-changing experience led me to discover customer mindset, a holistic understanding of your customer, and the first of two essential lessons that form the foundation of *Differentiated*. When you embrace your customer's mindset, you appreciate the intrinsic link between the rational and the emotional. You care about what your customer cares about. You realize that mindset determines what matters.

You might be wondering why I use the word customer in the context of an organization that is driven by purpose. There's a specific reason for it, and I'm anxious to explain why. But first, let's continue with why this mindset is crucial to differentiation.

The Declarative I

The typical strategy process frames the world from your point of view. Your organization is the I or we. You speak about your customers, your competitors, and your offerings. Your customers are little more than a circle in a Venn diagram. Your strategy process is designed around what your stakeholders consider important.

You get caught up listening to so many opinions because you're unsure of whose perspective matters most. Soon enough, the process is complete, just shy of inevitable fatigue. Everyone feels good about the result until this latest strategic plan finds itself on the shelf, another victim of the need to please and, dare I say, lack of strategic discipline. Who expected competition from so many different arenas, the erosion of market share blamed on branding when the problem was much more deeply rooted? Your organization had atrophied, and you didn't even know it. Your industry was morphing in unforeseen ways. The pandemic's ability to alter your course was an undeniable force.

Shifting customer preferences awakened competitive interests in your arena, some jumping in from disparate fields. Your customers had more options at their fingertips than ever before. Even worse, customers couldn't tell what differentiated your organization, and you didn't appreciate what mattered most to them. You'd been busy attending to stakeholders and deciphering trends, trying to listen for the signal through the noise. Everything important was categorized into four quadrants on your SWOT analysis—your organization's strengths, weaknesses, opportunities, and threats—taken into account.

Too Simple for the Times

We will pause our story so I can share an important insight. SWOT analysis has a critical flaw with strategic consequences for your organization. The ubiquitous tool lulls you into thinking your organization determines relevance. SWOT instills a false sense of confidence that what matters most to you matters most to your customer. SWOT can't lead you to differentiate your organization because it wasn't designed with a customer mindset.

Created more than fifty years ago when *Encyclopedia Britannica* presented the world's knowledge in a set of printed books, SWOT's simple framework was attuned to the times. Your organization was the declarative I. Back then, the shelf life for information was ten years or more. Today, information has the shelf life of a day, month, or year at best. Google is your connection to the world's ever-expanding body of knowledge, and your customer's lifeline to an increasing array of choices is only a keyword away. The Logan School knew that all too well. Let's rejoin them in the lunchroom.

A Radical Reframing

Imagine for a moment you are in The Logan School's lunchroom, experiencing your own epiphany thanks to understanding the customer mindset. No longer are you looking at the student from the school's, headmaster's, board member's, teacher's, or founder's perspective. You are the student looking at Logan and wondering what makes it the right fit for you.

You see it clearly now. The spotlight has swung to showcase the new lead. Your organization isn't the declarative I. The first person in your strategy narrative belongs to the person whose life you promise to impact through mission delivery.

It isn't enough to shift thinking from what you do to why you matter. It's time to reframe perspective from what you do to why you matter to your customer. When you take this bold leap and view choice from your customer's perspective, the answers to these two questions become obvious. The spotlight reveals what matters most.

> **Why does your organization matter?**
> **Why should it matter to me?**

These two questions go to the core of your quest for mission relevance because every time customers consider your organization, they ask themselves those questions. Their responses determine your organization's financial sustainability. Your customers become the declarative I.

The lead role has passed to another player. Your organization's view isn't the focal point of your next strategy process. It's time to emphasize a new voice. It's time to center your strategy around the person with the power to decide if your organization is substantially differentiated or even relevant.

Cue the cinematographer. Differentiation Zone places your customer at the center of your strategy process and the heart of your strategic plan.

Unleashing the Power of Customer Mindset

Customer mindset will lead to your breakthrough, as it did to mine. Numerous scholars and practitioners speak to the importance of customer perspective and experience, but no one else brings customer mindset to the center of your strategy like Differentiation Zone.

As you've learned, we aren't simply appreciating your customer's experience. We are looking at choice through their lens to understand how your organization compares and what makes it unique. These steps are essential to crafting a successful differentiation strategy.

> What does customer mindset mean for strategy?
> Everything. What matters most to your
> customer matters most to you. Differentiation
> is determined by your customer.

A differentiation strategy driven by customer mindset elevates your customer to the organization level and positions you to craft a strategy with a powerful through line to mission-relevant success measures. You'll see customer mindset in action as you read vignettes featuring Swallow Hill Music, the Children's Museum of Denver at Marsico Campus, The Logan School for Creative Learning, the University of Denver College of Arts, Humanities & Social Sciences, and the University of Denver Ritchie School of Engineering and Computer Science.

Like you, the leaders of these organizations have worked tirelessly to address important strategic issues such as changing customer expectations, shifting competitive landscapes, and sweeping trends. They've addressed the realities of potential irrelevance, the consequences of catapulting competitors, and the imaginings of new futures, all of which led to embracing a core that makes them unique. Their differentiators range from the power of play and the innovative potential of the creative arts to the everyday joy of music and a belief that a kindergartener can drive their educational experience. I invite you to learn with me, as I've learned so much from them.

I hope your "aha" moment generates a deep appreciation for your customers, whoever they may be, and an understanding of what they believe to be essential for themselves. Then everything else will fall into place for your strategy process.

Customer Mindset Brings an Equity Perspective

Customer mindset shines a powerful spotlight on your customers, including those you haven't served well or at all. People of color and underrepresented communities claim their rightful place in your mission and your strategy. Their expectations, aspirations, and unmet needs are in full view, as the chapter vignettes illustrate.

As you embrace your customer, you'll find yourself addressing language that subconsciously embeds privilege with unintended consequences. Customer mindset exposes your potential inclination to consider donors as customers.

You aren't the declarative I and neither is your donor. Your customer is the protagonist in your organization's story. Your job is to fully appreciate them. Your organization's strategic relevance depends on it.

It's time to change the strategy narrative. Welcome to Differentiation Zone.

A Note About COVID-19: At the time this book was published, we were in a worldwide distortion of unforeseeable effects and long-term consequences. Differentiation based on customer mindset has never been more important. Customers are reevaluating options and determining what matters most on a continuous basis. Empathy and appreciation are essential.

Creativity Meets Strategy

Differentiation Zone wasn't created in a lab with a hypothesis and research plan. Nor was it based on retrospective research on data sets. I'd considered a doctoral degree, and once I realized it involved statistics, I decided to double down on my commitment to mastering strategy in real time and in real life. When your work spans different fields like mine does, and you frequently find yourself doing something for the first time, your career is filled with opportunities for mastery.

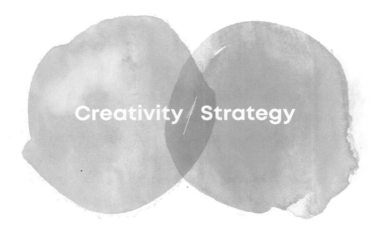

Each strategy engagement represents a promise from me to my customer, a commitment to deliver a strategic plan that achieves results. Such plans include the 2030 Master Plan for the Children's Museum of Denver at Marsico Campus and the Keystone Strategic Plan for the College of Arts, Humanities & Social Sciences at the University of Denver. Their success is my success.

A commitment to delivering results for my customers led me to a career-defining discovery in 2018. A colleague and I were discussing the findings from a competitive analysis for The Logan School. The experience was visceral. I felt the insight's truth as I saw it in my mind's eye. Customer mindset drove the discovery. This was a breakthrough that we weren't even looking for.

Eureka! We'd pushed beyond the design of our tried-and-true tool: the Strategic Sweet Spot, a model David Collis and Michael G. Rukstad created. My team conducted a literature review in 2020 to see if anyone else had experienced a similar breakthrough while using the Strategic Sweet Spot. We wanted to know if someone had invented a model like Differentiation Zone. The answer was no.

Mastery led to a new discovery. We revealed conclusions that the Sweet Spot tool wasn't designed to produce. Spoiler alert: we received a standing ovation from The Logan School faculty and staff following our lunchroom presentation.

A New Way Forward

Customer mindset changes everything. It inspired me to invent new tools for your strategy process. For example, I realized that the classic approach of classifying competitors as direct, indirect, and substitute didn't reflect customer mindset. Your customer isn't interested in industry or market, and they aren't making decisions based on those delineators, either. Other go-to tools such as SWOT and PEST were created prior to the

customer zeitgeist and don't incorporate your customer's perspective. I've made the leap for you.

As you get to know me, you'll learn that abstract painting propels my professional creativity and risk-taking, as it fuels my soul. Artists look at the world differently, and creativity opens a new portal. Years of painting have taught me to get out of my own way, not to tell myself no, and be open to the power of flow. I wouldn't have discovered Differentiation Zone without it. I invested ten thousand hours so you don't have to.

I am the first strategist to craft a differentiation strategy using a customer mindset. Soon you'll craft one, too.

Who Should Read This Book?

This book is designed for strategically minded individuals—such as executives, board members, consultants, and senior staff—committed to accelerating success for purpose-driven organizations. It is suited for people who appreciate strategy and those looking for current thinking and fresh approaches optimized for today's realities.

Differentiation Zone is inclusive of all organizations committed to mission delivery. It is indifferent to tax status; it isn't more appropriate for one funding model rather than another. At first glance, you may think it a better fit for earned-income organizations rather than those with business models reliant on financial contributions. As we know, grantmakers and philanthropists care a lot about differentiation, too.

Grab your highlighter and mobile device or laptop. I encourage you to engage in real-time exploration of concepts, tools, and case studies. Are you curious to learn more about the results achieved by the organizations exemplified here? Check out their websites. Read their plans, reports, and press releases. Keep a notebook to capture your learnings for an organization near and dear to you. You never know when an "aha" moment will strike. I'd be ready, if I were you.

My Strategy Declaration

I don't know about you, but I've never had a purpose-driven leader say to me, "We want to compete on cost." No one has declared to me that their strategy would center on being the low-cost provider in their mission area or serving as the Amazon or Walmart of food banks, museums, or schools.

Before we go further, let's clarify a point of confusion for many. Too often, the word strategy is used synonymously with tactic. But this is not the case. Your strategy is your organization's long-range direction or game plan. A tactic is a specific action to accomplish your strategy.

I've been privy to numerous conversations during which executives and board members have noted the importance of standing out and bemoaned the challenge of demonstrating uniqueness. The examples are prevalent and far-ranging, from higher education, K-12 education, human services, the arts, and more. This is especially true for 501(c)(3) nonprofits whose success has been tied to their ability to deliver unique services that meet a compelling need with proven results.

Let's begin with Michael Porter's seminal work on strategy. Porter's three pillars—cost, differentiation, and focus—have informed strategy design for decades. As noted above, a cost-only strategy seldom applies to organizations driven by purpose. It's also difficult to make the case for a focus-only strategy in the social sector. Even organizations that deliver comparable services across multiple locations, such as a food bank, don't use a one-size-fits-all approach to mission delivery. They realize the importance of tailoring to local community needs, which accentuates the effectiveness of a differentiation strategy.

I'd go so far as to say that differentiation is the strategy of choice for organizations driven by purpose. Looking back, I realize that every strategic plan I've written had a differentiation strategy. Every. One. And every strategic plan I've read stakes their organization's future on differentiation in the marketplace.

What is essential to consider as we redefine differentiation? It all begins with the Six Guiding Principles.

How Is This Book Organized?

Get ready for discovery. I've divided your journey into two sections, each with its own vignettes and markers. I've mapped the route for you. Along the way, I'll share stories from my journey.

Get ready to:

+ Explore Differentiation Zone through its Six Guiding Principles in section 1 and the Four-Step Process in section 2.
+ Delve into real-world stories of organizations and the people who care about them.
+ Revisit classic concepts with a new appreciation for their relevance to your organization.
+ Build a portfolio of new tools and up-to-date methods based on the latest thinking.

Section 1
Embrace Your Customer's Mindset

Originality in View

Many months transpired between my eureka moment with The Logan School, as I mentioned in the Introduction, and the white paper that preceded this book. In late 2018, I reminded myself that I might be onto something and that it deserved my attention. It was also vital to safeguard the intellectual property (IP). I endeavored to keep that promise to myself as I engaged a small circle of trusted advisors to help me move the IP forward in early 2019.

In March 2019, I spent a week writing in Southern California. The Six Guiding Principles first appeared on paper then, and that same week the word mindset appeared in context. The flash in my mind's eye transported to paper.

Strategy development is, by nature, an iterative and creative process. Various inputs come together in the form of research findings, future forecasts, opinions, perspectives, and aspirations on a quest for true insights. To paraphrase the design firm IDEO's definition of insight, it is an original conclusion that makes someone sit up and take notice. That quest for authentic insights led to the epiphany that is Differentiation Zone.

I reverse engineered ten years of creative experience to reveal the essential truths that guide my work. This is what I've always done. Now I'm declaring it as mine.

True differentiation in the marketplace is based on originality. It is the realization that what we have to offer to the world is unparalleled and unique. This idea takes me back to the beginning. We were huddled over my colleague's desk when it struck me. Our pursuit of clarity for The Logan School crystallized my thinking. Everything came together with a new focus.

Your New Mantra

Your Differentiation Zone process is driven by the Six Guiding Principles. We'll explore them one by one in this section of your book. They are foundational to your new mantra—your customer mindset—and the evolution of your strategic perspective.

You've likely already noticed that I believe in the word "customer." Don't worry if your eyes roll a bit. I've seen the smirks before. The word might be off-putting for some, for whom it sounds commercial or transactional. It might even rub *you* the wrong way or appear to go against your values. Or you might feel it reduces an important relationship to a financial exchange. You didn't go into business, after all; you went into the nonprofit arena or chose to set up an enterprise driven by purpose or work in higher education, schools, outdoor recreation, or museums. For you, it's about the mission. Here's the thing: it's about mission for me, too, as you'll read in "Principle One: It's All About the Customer."

> **Your customer is the person whose life you promise to impact through mission delivery.**

The concept of customer raises a corollary dilemma as well, so brace yourself for "Principle Two: Not Every Stakeholder Is a Customer." Take a breath and put down your highlighter. Drop the pen. I saw you write that sassy comment in the margin. You can come back to it later.

Some of you will readily relate to "Principle Three: Competition Is Prevalent" because it makes it obvious that your competitive landscape is changing. "Principle Four: Your Environment Creates Context, Not Focus" inspires fresh thinking and an "Oh, I hadn't thought of that." You'll say goodbye to SWOT and PEST. "Principle Five: You Compete in More Than One Industry" is best illustrated in action. Some people immediately feel the power of "Principle Six: Watch Out for the Zone of Indifference" since they bring personal experience to bear and a sense that, "Yeah, that doesn't really matter to me."

Six Guiding Principles of Differentiation Zone

Principle One: It's All About the Customer. Clarity of customer is essential to mission relevance and strategic differentiation. After all, if you aren't sure who you serve, you won't achieve the impact you promise or the success you desire.

Principle Two: Not Every Stakeholder Is a Customer. Avoid the temptation to include every stakeholder category in your definition of customer—your staff, board, volunteers, and partners among them. While they're important, they aren't your customer.

Principle Three: Competition Is Prevalent. You can't afford to ignore the realities of never-ending competition in the customer zeitgeist. Your customer defines your competitive set without you ever knowing it.

Principle Four: Your Environment Creates Context, Not Focus. Focus on the small set of factors most likely to influence behaviors and drive choices for customers and competitors. Other factors may be interesting but are unlikely to shape their actions or drive your future direction.

Principle Five: You Compete in More Than One Industry. The lines demarking industries have blurred to the point of irrelevance, freeing you to consider the myriad industries in which you actually compete.

Principle Six: Watch Out for the Zone of Indifference. Your customer doesn't really care about some of the features you hold dear, and you certainly don't want to build your strategy around them.

Differentiation Zone grew out of an insight centered around the customer, embodied in "Principle One: It's All About the Customer." By design, "Principle Six: Watch Out for the Zone of Indifference" brings you back to your customer. Together we'll explore them in chapters 1 through 6, concluding each with essential learnings.

1.

Principle One: It's All About the Customer

The Power of Play

There you are, having the time of your life, the wind blowing through your hair, a sword in hand, and a cape on your back. Cue the Wonder Woman theme song. Next up, the giant bubble machine. But wait! Should we fly paper airplanes, shop for groceries, make stuff from scrap wood, or go outside over the hill past the families eating their lunches in the grass to the aerial obstacle course aptly named Adventure Forest? You might be four years old, fourteen, thirty-four, or sixty-four. It doesn't matter. It's a one-size-fits-all cape. The wonders and joys of childhood have no age limit.

The Children's Museum of Denver at Marsico Campus is the rare kind of place that gives people of all ages permission to play. The Children's Museum lives at the intersection of education and experience. Of fun-filled learning. Of learning fueled by play. Of free, unstructured, be-a-kid play. The sort of play that was commonplace decades ago, before Barney morphed into Teletubbies, then Disney+. When parents felt safe letting their children stay out until dinner time. Free play is essential to early childhood development and the formation of personal agency. The realization from a young age that each of us has the inherent power to decide, and the ability to act. To be the heroes of our own stories.

I've known the leadership team for years through projects we've done together and through leadership and community work. Their commitment to data-driven, long-range planning is evident in their success and and in their courageous leadership. They have a deep respect for children and believe every child deserves to be the hero of their own story.

I was thrilled when in 2017 they asked me to assist them in creating a strategic plan that would encompass programs, facilities, and the campus. They had bravely steered through the 2009 recession to raise millions for an expansion, guided by the fact that theirs was the most crowded museum for children in the country. That boldness found its way onto our master planning task force. Board and volunteer leadership pushed us to think beyond a mere five years. We envisioned 2040 to create a plan for 2030. It was audacious, yet liberating, to consider what may be. Our realization: today's four-year-old is the parent of 2040.

I found myself at the museum at least once a month for meetings. Customer mindset came too. I observed their mission in real life and experienced it as a guest during after-hours events for the twenty-one and older set. The museum primarily serves children from newborn to age eight, and their caregivers. A popular destination for Colorado families with young children, it is a busy place, with infants in carriers or strollers, unstable toddlers learning to walk, and older kids of ages five or so accompanied by adults.

I absorbed everything I was sensing and learning. My lived experience with The Logan School had taught me to spot novel insights and fresh thinking about mission delivery. I could see blind spots they missed. And I held firm in the belief that the museum had the potential to deliver more mission impact for the diverse and growing community. Comprehensive customer data revealed what customers cared about, including underserved members of the community. During many months and numerous conversations, the planning task force toggled back and forth between realities and possibilities. As consultants, we sought to propel the museum beyond current constraints to appreciate what mattered most to their customers today and what was likely to matter even more in a future with abundant options.

In the middle of that conversation was this essential question: whose life was the museum promising to impact through mission delivery? There was an opportunity to positively affect personal agency over a lifetime. Was the mission exclusive to families with young children, or might there be room for expansive thinking? What more could the museum offer adult visitors? And older kids? People craved opportunities to have fun together as families and sought experiences filled with love and positive connections.

Your Customer Is the Person Whose Life You Promise to Impact Through Mission Delivery

A strategy process is an ideal time to reaffirm or recalibrate your organization's mission. My approach has been strongly influenced by Peter Drucker's work with organizations, most notably his thinking about mission and customer. I believe in the fundamental power of mission and the inextricable link between your mission and your customer. You can't achieve clarity of one without the other.

My favorite mission question delivers a both-and solution. "What difference do you make in the lives of those you serve?" I love this mission question because it calls out two essentials: what difference and for whom. What difference invites deliberation about your organization's true purpose and the effects on your customers. For whom asks you to clarify the customer you promise to impact through mission delivery. You want to matter most to the people who matter most to you—your customers.

The corollary—"How do you know?"—connects mission with outcomes and organizational success measures. With your statement of strategy, you create powerful alignment. Your mission, strategy, and success measures are guided by customer mindset.

As my team and the museum's task force talked through future possibilities, emboldened as we imagined to 2040, we faced the challenge: who was the museum not reaching? While record numbers of families were being served, were some being left behind? How could the museum extend its impact? The task force wouldn't let go of these questions. They kept coming up during meetings. Conversations turned to bored older kids, the unmet needs of children with disabilities, families whose native language wasn't English, and kids joined by large extended families. We couldn't help but notice distracted adults whiling away the time on their phones as they waited for their kids. The power of consumer culture found its way into the museum.

You Can't Escape the Customer Zeitgeist

The sweep and pace of change are breathtaking. Broad consumer trends quickly become widely adopted norms. TikTok overtakes Hollywood as the preferred source of content for young people. Why watch someone else's story when you can direct your own? Customer mindset pinpoints the competitive advantage. It was only a matter of time before the grownups flocked there, too.

Differentiation Zone recognizes what Malcolm Gladwell called a tipping point. A tipping point signifies how small actions at the right time, in the right place, and with the right people create a movement. As energy and momentum sustain over time, a tip over to the new occurs. The old is left behind. It's easy to recognize a tipping point after it has occurred. Global societies, especially those in advanced economies, are defined by the ability to curate our lives on our own terms. This time, the tip is fueled by a device that fits comfortably in the palm of our hands.

Your customers are searching and exploring without you even knowing about it. And they are redefining your competitive set, too, as you'll learn in chapters 3 and 7. Welcome to the customer zeitgeist. Your customers are dialed in 24/7 and 365 days a year. "Why?" is the recording running in the back of their minds. That was true before the pandemic and even more so today when online is our lifeline.

Everyone experiences unique products and services from an increasing variety of providers. The list morphs every day as new entrants move in.

These providers may be nonprofit, for-profit, or something in between like a B Corporation or an L3C. From the movies you stream and the organic groceries you buy online, to the university you attend and the home office where you're meeting virtually, you choose products and services because they matter to you. And you likely don't care a wit about tax status, either.

Take note. Other strategy models don't recognize the tipping point and aren't designed to address the realities it holds for your customers and their choices. Now you have the language and tools to strategically make sense of it.

The tipping point held implications for the Children's Museum just as it does for your organization. The fact that you don't like these consumer trends and prefer to avoid social media doesn't alter reality. Smartphones fueled the tip. And we aren't going back. This is personal agency reinforced by the customer zeitgeist.

Your Customer Decides What Matters Most

Denver was becoming more global, more diverse, and more expensive. Families increasingly moved to surrounding cities with more affordable housing and new amenities. With longer commutes, they often found the parking lots packed with minivans and SUVs of other metro-area families and cultural tourists.

The museum's customers knew what mattered most to them. They loved the museum but not the crowds. They also loved what it offered for their young children and hoped for more joy and wonder for their older kids, and maybe something special for themselves, too. Families craved opportunities to learn and grow together beyond daytime hours. Evenings and weekends were better for working families, after all. They also sought a space that celebrated their cultures and honored their languages, one where they could see themselves reflected in staffing, amenities, and programs.

The Children's Museum couldn't afford to rest on its laurels. An expanding array of options were available to their customers who, if they couldn't find what they needed at the museum, could engage with others eager to take the museum's place online and in the community. These alternatives possessed advantages the museum did not, such as convenience and novelty.

The issue before the task force boiled down to these customer-centered questions: what if the museum could support young children in becoming the heroes of their own stories and, without compromising that deep commitment, extend the museum's impact to older children and grown-ups with equity, access, and inclusion embedded throughout?

Customer mindset ensured the 2030 Master Plan embodied the heartfelt desires of the museum's customers. From those early visits and conversations, throughout months of discovery and debate, the museum's board and staff grabbed the one-size-fits-all capes and cued the music. They faced the wind machine headlong into a shared aspiration to bring the power of play to more kids and grown-ups. Relevance was never taken for granted. Fresh thinking and dynamic learning made sure of it.

Customer Clarity Is Essential to Mission and Strategic Relevance

In this chapter, you learned what mattered most to the museum's customers and how that revelation inspired original insights about mission and differentiation in the marketplace. Museum leadership didn't shy away from the big questions or turn away from a word like

> Your customer is the person whose life you promise to impact through mission delivery.

relevance, one that is often overused, relegated to the jargon bin, and discarded out of turn.

When something is relevant, it is important to the matter at hand. Importance leads you to significance. Your path to sustained significance begins with clarity of customer. Let the museum's story be your guide. You learned how clarity of customer catalyzed the museum's leadership team members to confidently examine their mission for continued relevance. In doing so, they redoubled their commitment and, taking a big gulp, promised to extend the power of play to more kids and families.

"Principle One: It's All About the Customer" invited you to appreciate customer mindset from the beginning of your strategy process. You'll read about the full power of the Children's Museum's differentiation strategy in chapter 9. It's a wonderful example of how a differentiation strategy driven by customer mindset elevates your customer to the organization level and allows you to craft a strategy with a powerful through line to mission-relevant success measures.

Before we leap too far ahead, allow me to share a final point about customers. Each of us is a person in the world engaging with organizations on our own terms. We don't label ourselves as members, donors, stakeholders, program participants, or the like. Your organization does. This is another example of the tendency to make your organization the declarative I.

Achieving customer clarity requires that we address the ideas in "Principle Two: Not Every Stakeholder Is a Customer." Ready your highlighter and your pen. I'm sure you'll have a lot to say about it.

ESSENTIAL LEARNINGS

Principle One: It's All About the Customer

1. Your customer is the person whose life you promise to impact through mission delivery.
2. You can't escape the customer zeitgeist.
3. Your customer decides what matters most to them.
4. Customer clarity is essential to mission and strategic relevance.

2.

Principle Two: Not Every Stakeholder Is a Customer

Cue the Furrowed Brows

I was just in time for the dean's monthly meeting with the department chairs. A discussion about strategic planning was next on the agenda. And my job was to relay the importance of customer clarity. I was ready for the furrowed brows and unhappy expressions. The discreet head shaking. Those visual signals would be a precursor to the verbal expressions that would follow. They were faculty, after all, so I knew to expect an argument or two. Doctoral programs trained them to take a stand; debate was in their DNA.

The flash of recognition was instantaneous. I'm sure they were asking themselves whether I was serious when I said they weren't the customer. How could I dare to speak the word "customer" at all? I was suggesting the student was the college's customer. Oh no. More downward glances. This was going to be rough. Thank goodness they were sticklers for time management and the meeting would soon be over.

I'd done my job. I'd raised the issue and noted the requirement. The college's strategic plan would be vetted by the university administration and approved by the board of trustees. The university was looking for a compelling narrative that proclaimed differentiation, a plan that would raise capital and sustain competitive advantage. I knew what we had to do.

Thank goodness we had a few more months in our process and a dean skilled in consensus building. Both would prove to be invaluable in achieving the success that is the Keystone Strategic Plan for the College of Arts, Humanities & Social Sciences at the University of Denver. The faculty would discover they have an appetite for bold thinking. Their vision: To be a leader in creating the future of a liberal and creative arts education. Their strategy: to revolutionize a liberal and creative arts education. It was the first time I'd written revolutionize in a strategic plan.

But I'm getting ahead of myself. Many faculty dismissed the word customer, and some downright despised it. They protested that the word implies that getting an education is nothing more than a commercial transaction. Prepare for the furrowing of brows.

For decades, university strategic plans were internally focused, more akin to an accreditation review than a strategic road map—one team of faculty reviewing another and asking questions about topics of mutual interest. The notion of strategy was anathema for many. Wasn't higher education focused on knowledge creation and scholarship? Weren't the faculty the customers?

Then the narrative shifted. Supply exceeded demand, resulting in a fight for market position. *US News & World Report* rankings were ubiquitous. Everyone was trying to move up the ladder in an effort to garner market share. Rankings were an attempt to provide comparison data to prospective customers. Quality attracted quality and rankings mattered a lot. They still do.

The new narrative recognizes that the twentieth-century model is inadequate to the task of preparing graduates for the careers and communities of tomorrow, which brings us back to customers and stakeholders.

The ten thousand hours of experience I mentioned in the introduction led to two essential lessons. I've already introduced customer mindset. Now it's time to share the other.

The essence of your strategy is choice.

I stood resolute with the faculty. Years of wrestling for consensus from board members and executives had taught me to focus on the essentials embodied in the Six Guiding Principles. I knew to take a stand. You can't craft an effective differentiation strategy without clarity of customer.

If we want our customer to choose our organization over other options, then we must focus on them. Without a laser focus and the consensus-based process to achieve it, we'll find ourselves trapped in trade-offs. Should we satisfy the faculty or the board? The volunteer, alumnus, or donor? How does the customer fit into it all? More on that in chapters 7 and 8.

Here's the thing. You get to choose. Which customers will you impact? How will you serve them in novel ways? How will you achieve strategic differentiation for your organization?

Those answers will lead you to clarity of customer. Achieving customer clarity and working through concepts like customer segments, personas, and market niches means you have to address the fact that not every stakeholder is a customer.

Principle One: It's All About the Customer.

Principle Two: Not Every Stakeholder Is a Customer.

Principle Three: Competition Is Prevalent.

Principle Four: Your Environment Creates Context, Not Focus.

Principle Five: You Compete in More Than One Industry.

Principle Six: Watch Out for the Zone of Indifference.

Your Customer Is a Unique Stakeholder

Let's consider the obvious. We could replace faculty with curators, social workers, environmentalists, educators, or board members and find ourselves where we started—disagreeing about the customer. Believe me, I've been met with the same pursed lips and arguments during workshops, attendees smiling as they shake their heads.

The word stakeholder is often used as a catchall to embrace individuals important to organizations. But a desire to include everyone in our orbit and treat them with care muddles thinking. Confusion is reinforced by the widespread adoption of concepts like customer service to donors and volunteers, for example, until the word customer becomes watered down, too.

Your customer is the only stakeholder whose life you promise to impact through mission delivery. Your mission, programs, outcomes, and strategy are centered around your customer. Everyone else helps make that promise a reality. Their roles and their commitments are different.

The narrative has changed. Not every stakeholder is a customer.

We spoke to the importance of customer clarity in chapter 1 and noted the link between customer, mission, and relevance.

Your Donor Is Not Your Customer

When I ask people to think about who their customers are, they respond with a question, such as, "Aren't you talking about beneficiaries?" and my mind races for a response. Then the flash. For someone to be the beneficiary, someone else has to be the benefactor and, by extension, a donor and a receiver.

Here's the catch. The language of benefactor-beneficiary reinforces an established power structure based on privilege. Without a second thought, you just elevated your donor to customer status, implying that your promise of mission impact extends to them as well. The proclivity to follow the money causes mission drift and derails your differentiation efforts. Then we're back to "Principle One: It's All About the Customer" as we attempt to untangle who's who.

> Your customer is the person whose life you promise to impact through mission delivery.

You may rail against the word customer because it leaves you wondering who you are. Let's keep it simple. Yours is an organization committed to delivering mission impact.

Your customer is a person with a name like Rosa, Ibrahim, or Pat. They don't self-identify as a program participant or a beneficiary. That's your lingo, not theirs. They are clear about who they are. Are you?

Your Stakeholders Contribute to Mission Delivery

What about your employees, volunteers, board members, alumni, donors, and partners? Each is a vital contributor to mission delivery who provides time, talent, and treasure. You couldn't do what you do without them. They aren't the beneficiaries of mission impact. They are not your customer.

Stakeholders are an important resource in your Differentiation Zone process. They generate ideas and serve as a sounding board. Some comprise the board of directors with fiduciary responsibility for strategic decisions. Staff, partners, and influencers bring a critical understanding of customers and competitors. They provide input and feedback during the discovery process. Their voices, expertise, and diverse views matter. Your stakeholders vouchsafe the uniqueness of your differentiators and the soundness of your strategy. If the strategic insights don't resonate with stakeholders, then there's a good chance they aren't original and authentic. Just ask The Logan School or the University of Denver.

Higher education, like other purpose-driven industries, is full of stakeholders such as employees, board members, partners, volunteers, donors, and communities. The broader the array of stakeholders and the more complex the decision-making process, the more likely we are to be confused about who's who.

Embracing a customer mindset helps to make sense of it. Mastery of thought leads to calling the question and honoring strategic direction in service to your mission and customer.

Who's Who?

It's easy to feel confused about the customer when multiple stakeholders are involved. Rest assured, you only have one customer—the person whose life you promise to impact through mission delivery.

Let's use higher education to illuminate the differences.

+ **Your customer is the person whose life you promise to impact through mission delivery.** If you enroll them, grade them, and graduate them, then they are your customer. The recipient of an internship or scholarship? Ditto.

+ **Decision makers may be involved, too.** These are the parents and family members of your customer. Or they may be an employer paying for a certificate, course, or degree. Decision makers may receive secondary benefits of mission delivery. But they aren't sitting in your class hoping to pass. Decision makers are looking to you to deliver mission impact for the person who matters to them—their employee or family member. That person matters most to you too.

+ **Donors share your commitment to mission impact.** Your organization provides the vehicle through which they achieve their goals. They believe in your strategy, contribute funding to your business model, and champion your mission. Their name on the scholarship catalyzed your customer's academic career.

+ **Influencers have leverage over resources, reputation, and access.** They may be government officials, savvy executives, neighborhood associations, foundation program officers, donors, or well-connected community members. Some volunteers and board members have additional influence beyond your organization, given their networks and reach. They agree to informational interviews knowing your customer is looking for a job lead.

+ **Partners are part of your business model.** They bring the necessary expertise, resources, and skills to ensure mission delivery is effective. They are committed to success for your customers. They may be internship placements or community research sites. They aren't in cap and gown, anticipating a diploma.

+ **Your board, staff, and volunteers are committed to mission impact, too.** They are vital to customer success. But they aren't counting on career services to connect them with a great job.

Trouble awaits when there is a disconnect between your customer's desired outcomes and the expectations of decision makers, influencers, donors, or partners. One expects A while the other hopes for the promise of B. Alignment is your aim. Without it, you won't realize your promised outcomes, and your Competitors' Edge will be diminished.

Quiz: You Know They Aren't a Customer If . . .

I developed this simple quiz to help you convert a sassy smirk into an "aha" moment. You know they aren't a customer if you can check off more than one of these characteristics.

1. They have a job description.
    - ⬤ Employee
    - ⬤ Volunteer
    - ⬤ Board member

2. You evaluate their job performance.
    - ⬤ Employee
    - ⬤ Volunteer
    - ⬤ Board member

3. They can be let go.
    - ⬤ Employee
    - ⬤ Volunteer
    - ⬤ Board member
    - ⬤ Partner

4. Their relationship with your organization is governed by federal, state, or local laws or regulations such as workers' compensation.
    - ⬤ Employee
    - ⬤ Volunteer
    - ⬤ Board member

5. Your relationship with them is controlled by a contract, agreement, or memorandum of understanding.
    - ⬤ Donor
    - ⬤ Partner

6. You have risk management protocols and insurance policies in place to safeguard your organization against risk, such as workplace injury or directors' and officers' liability.
    - ⬤ Employee
    - ⬤ Volunteer
    - ⬤ Board member

7. You hope they will influence the decisions of your customer.
    - ⬤ Decision maker
    - ⬤ Influencer
    - ⬤ Donor

Here's the final clue. Your success is measured by your customer's success. That's the clearest signal of all.

Now that we've established how your strategy must focus on the customer and how to discern who your customer is and isn't, it's time to turn our attention to "Principle Three: Competition Is Prevalent." As we'll explore in chapter 3, you have ready access to insights about the competition. That's right—we're talking about your customer.

ESSENTIAL LEARNINGS

Principle Two: Not Every Stakeholder Is a Customer

1. Your customer is a unique stakeholder.
2. Your donor is not your customer.
3. Your stakeholders contribute to mission delivery.

3.

Principle Three: Competition Is Prevalent

Bears and Blockchain, Oh My!

The energy was palpable. Parents and grandparents navigated the hallways and reconfigured classrooms in route to visit student booths. The range of topics was extraordinary, from ballet and artificial intelligence to bugs. Look, there's a display on astrophysics and one on blackchain. Each student's portfolio was a unique mix of models, posters, and PowerPoint slide decks. Paint and pipe cleaners, too. It was a marvel to hear a seven-year-old describe everything they'd learned about bear habitats, including a mathematical model they'd designed to predict encroachment on new housing areas.

The Logan School's EXPO was as remarkable as promised, with passion, talent, and uniqueness on full display. Teachers were close enough to show support but didn't manage the interaction. Each child directed their own learning experience.

Adults milled about, enthralled by their students' accomplishments while happily witnessing the success of others. The school culture cemented shared experiences as well as the rites and rituals passed on to the newest families. No wonder word-of-mouth advertising was so important. So was the legacy of alumni selecting Logan for their children. I imagined being the parent of a Logan student. There was my child, beaming with pride, having learned so much about bears and blockchain.

Prior to EXPO, I'd attended a reception for prospective families. School staff, current students, and parents greeted parents with kids in tow. The parents mentally noted these strengths and concerns:

I'd heard of Logan throughout the years from friends whose kids attended the school. They spoke of the challenge of finding the right school for their kiddo, the pain of a poor fit on their faces followed quickly by a smile of relief when Logan proved to be the right choice. I kept going back to something the head of school shared with me. One sentence pulled it all together, its truth inescapable: "A gifted child isn't gifted just one hour a day." It seemed like a no-brainer after months of study. Other schools weren't tailor-made in the same way as Logan.

What happened when a family didn't "get" Logan? Then the questions followed about learning and preparation for high school. Time was of the essence. Other schools were encroaching on Logan's target market, and the school's differentiation was unclear.

> Your customer is the person whose life you promise to impact through mission delivery.

Sensing the need to convey what made Logan distinctive, school leadership promised to deliver the gift of clarity to the school community. It was vital that Logan name and claim its unique market position as the optimal choice for a gifted student. Pushback against the term gifted and a misunderstanding of the needs, attributes, and off-the-charts capabilities of these students make the task of selling a school designed specifically for them even more difficult. And then there's the social consciousness around inclusion. Logan did not want to appear exclusive.

In-person observations and customer feedback illustrated an unavoidable truth: too many prospective parents had a hard time distinguishing Logan from other independent schools.

Competitors Are Inescapable

Logan's competitive landscape had changed dramatically with the proliferation of independent schools, charter schools, high-performing public schools, and public schools tailored to prodigies in the arts and sciences, each with its own compelling brand and suite of programs. The specific needs of gifted students motivated more schools to adjust the programming and messaging needed to attract them. Public schools were as committed to differentiation as private schools, and all of them pursued the same markers of success: successful students and engaged families with the capacity for fundraising. Every principal turned into a CEO.

A customer mindset sheds light on the selection and decision-making process. It was a daunting landscape to navigate. Prospective families filled months with school tours, meetings, and late-night internet sleuthing. Mommy blogs, extended family, and co-workers were generous with recommendations. The list of options would narrow to two, then three. When would a family find the one for them?

A confused parent is a stressed parent, and stressed parents often go for the safe or obvious choice. Millennial and Gen Z parents rely on social media, video streaming, and word-of-mouth referrals from friends. It didn't matter if boomer parents and their friends loved Logan and were willing to recommend it if those same people weren't engaging with younger parents.

Stories like this one occur every day as customers navigate options. They decide when, how, and where to engage with your mission. Don't let a disdain for competition lull you into thinking that you aren't battling for heart, mind, and market share. Quite the opposite. You compete with players you've never met and don't know anything about. Your customer is dialed in even if you are not, due to the power of Google and readily accessible online resources.

Analyze Competitors with a Customer Mindset

When options abound, and information overload is the norm, it's challenging to sort through it all to discover who can deliver what matters most. The essential truths reveal themselves through a holistic human-centered approach; customer mindset illuminates the full humanity of gifted students and the realities their parents face. Making the right choice about education can be especially difficult for parents when their gifted child can't turn their talents on or off during the school day (or any day, for that matter) and often struggle to fit in. They are who they are 24/7 and 365 days a year. These students need a school designed with them in mind. A school that understands them and loves them unconditionally. A school that trusts them to drive their learning experience, beginning at four-and-a-half years old.

Achieving this depth of understanding about what mattered most and what made Logan stand out in the marketplace necessitated a new approach to analyzing competitors. After all, we weren't looking at other schools designed specifically for Logan's niche market. The school was aware of fourteen other schools' moves, each vying to serve this growth market. We needed to understand how other schools were appealing to kids and parents and where they had a Competitors' Edge over Logan.

Strategists were trained to classify competitors as direct, indirect, and substitute. Industry and market were the two defining attributes for categorization. That rubric worked when everyone stayed in their lanes. A public school offered a classic K-12 curriculum. Charters weren't prolific. And there wasn't an abundance of independent schools morphing to meet an expanded market need. Other schools were savvy in recognizing that families were hungry for more choices. They'd switched into Logan's lane and traffic was heavy. These other options weren't mere substitutes. There was innovation and a dash of the unexpected. What were parents and kids responding to? How were they evaluating options?

We discovered a fresh approach to classifying competitors based on customer mindset. As you'll recall, Logan's singular distinction was revealed by rigorous competitor analysis. You'll learn more about our new framework for analyzing competitors in chapter 7. You'll meet the world of replacements, alternatives, catapults, and community builders. Customer mindset illuminated the usual suspects and new players as we sought to understand who was moving in with novel offerings and who sought to serve Logan's students as part of a larger school community for families seeking options that could meet all of their children's needs on a single campus.

The Comparison Never Ends

How do you stack up against these newly defined competitors? The old categories of direct, indirect, and substitute can't guide you to the answers you seek. They were designed for a simpler time. You need a clear-eyed view of competitors—and not just the ones in plain sight.

You can't assume that what differentiated you last year is still true today. Your dialed-in customer is absorbing information in real time as your competitors adjust to new market realities. How do you stack up?

+ Can you be easily replaced?
+ Are there alternatives with features you don't offer?
+ Are innovators catapulting into your market?

As we'll discover in chapter 4, your context drives competitor actions and customer choices. Focus on forces with the greatest potential to shape your future or risk becoming simply ordinary as competitors grab an edge. Your guide is "Principle Four: Your Environment Creates Context, Not Focus."

ESSENTIAL LEARNINGS

Principle Three: Competition Is Prevalent

1. Competitors are inescapable.
2. Analyze competitors with a customer mindset.
3. The comparison never ends.

4.

Principle Four: Your Environment Creates Context, Not Focus

Gale-Force Winds Ahead

You recalled the view with fondness; your desk was placed just so to take it in. The days were breathtaking when Mount Evans was capped in snow, the quintessential blue sky of Colorado serving as its backdrop. Too bad you couldn't enjoy the vista as often as you anticipated. Your time was consumed by a growing list of fast-moving issues. The day's Twitter feed occupied more time than you imagined.

You knew the statistics when you'd accepted the promotion. Deans and presidents frequently turned over after five years, having attempted to balance annual and long-range fundraising requirements with evolving customer and community expectations and the unique culture of tenured faculty. A polarized political climate and movements such as #MeToo, #BlackLivesMatter, and #ClimateStrike created expectations that institutions like yours take a stand.

Fortunately, the economy was expanding year over year—good, although nothing to write home about—and jobs awaited your graduates in key industries and growth markets. Donors could be courted to fund endowments, scholarships, innovation centers, and new buildings. As employers competed for talent, some decided that a degree wasn't a requirement after all. Students were enticed to go to campuses with hotel-quality amenities, a visible return for the high cost of tuition, and inevitable student-loan debt. Your new buildings would be underway soon.

Everyone knew the obvious but not what to do about it. Academia was running headlong into the future yet hadn't changed in notable ways for centuries. Yes, universities were attempting to manage costs by shifting to adjuncts from full-time faculty and increasing the variety of degree offerings. There were nods to online education, mobile-friendly student supports, and alternative credentialing, but much of that innovation happened along the fringes of the industry, led by upstarts like Khan Academy.

Your national association kept you apprised of it all. Colleges and universities could see the approaching storm. A declining population of traditional-age students meant there was an oversupply of product. Supply exceeded demand, especially in the liberal and creative arts. The media was awash in stories about virtual reality, driverless cars, and the potential of 5G. Job-ready degrees in science, technology, engineering, and math were the rage. None of that was possible without creative thinking, risk taking, and the ability to imagine.

The headwind was growing stronger as you looked to 2025. Numerous data sources pointed to the upcoming challenges. While institutions with best-in-class reputations, stellar brands, and enviable endowments were expected to survive, the small overly leveraged private colleges sprinkled in cities and towns across the United States weren't expected to fare as well. The long-awaited shakeout was beginning. Your institution had its own transformation strategy.

The storm was preceded by questions about return on investment (ROI) and expectations that universities meet civic missions, too. Simultaneously, everyone was striving to serve the Gen Z student market, with its unique mix of expectations and diverse populations, many of whom were the first in their families to attend college.

This was higher education's backdrop.

The stakes were high for the College of Art, Humanities & Social Sciences at the University of Denver, as described in chapter 2. The new strategic plan needed to galvanize donors, partners, and alumni to better serve the evolving student customer. It was also a time to clearly demark the college's customer from the abundance of stakeholders. The college couldn't afford to be distracted by the issue du jour or the politicized trend of little real consequence in five years. Those topics tended to take faculty down the rabbit hole while delaying vital conversations about customers and competitors.

Many in higher education believed a SWOT analysis was sufficient to understand the shifting landscape. SWOT, with its easy bracketing of strengths, weaknesses, opportunities, and threats, was shorthand for let's scan the environment. The process of completing the analysis was more important than the conclusions; the findings were crafted from ready evidence. The result was a four-quadrant matrix that could be condensed into two columns. Opportunities were synonymous with strengths, and threats sounded like strengths, too. Thank goodness we didn't have too many weaknesses.

Cue the consultant once again. Over the years, I'd trained myself to listen for the signal through the noise to spot the trends with the power to shape or drive an organization's future. After a brief scan of the analysis, I knew what was missing and what we couldn't afford to overlook if we were to create a powerful differentiation strategy. We needed to concentrate on the student experience and the changing expectations for life during and after college. The result? A revolutionary strategy informed by context. Customer mindset was the keystone.

The powerful forces driving change in higher education rippled across the social sector. I'd witnessed the same SWOT default, too—a tendency to use it without understanding the limitations and the process of grouping that was rooted in opinions rather than data and insights. Unfortunately, many executives make the mistake of compiling their organization's internal capabilities instead of investigating crucial shifts in customer preferences and competitor actions. The SWOT inventory exercise often places organizations squarely in the Zone of Indifference, as we'll discuss in chapter 6.

Goodbye, SWOT and PEST. Hello, Context

Old habits are hard to break. Let's remind ourselves of the inherent weaknesses of SWOT analysis. SWOT is analogous to a 1960s-era rotary phone. Your phone has evolved from a dial to Siri. In contrast, there is no SWOT 5.0. It remains unchanged, a metaphor for a simpler time. SWOT comforts you into thinking you've covered everything important. Repeated autopilot use has conditioned you to believe that a mere summary suffices for comprehending a dynamic and complex environment. It wasn't designed to spot connections across disparate issues, provoke fresh insights, or inspire breakthrough thinking. It aimed for basic categorization.

Consequently, SWOT leads you to oversimplify. You focus on your organization instead of your strategic context. Your board and staff can't help but focus there anyway. They need a tool that pulls them out of their comfort zone and deals with the consequential issues at hand.

Here's an example. I can't tell you how many times I've seen "We are the best-kept secret" listed as a threat and an opportunity. Let that sink in for a moment. That framing shifts your thinking from "Our competitors are encroaching on our market" and "Our customers can't tell us apart" to "We're great" and "More folks should know about us."

SWOT underestimates the effects of:

+ Broad societal trends, such as non-binary gender identification and new family structures
+ Sweeping consumer behaviors like the use of mobile payments
+ New competitor categories as described in chapter 3
+ Diminishing industry boundaries that we'll discuss in chapter 5
+ Customer disinterest in what you hold dear, which you'll learn about in chapter 6
+ Evolving economies as evidenced by the gig economy, sharing economy, and circular economy

These shortcomings draw our attention to the inherent drawbacks of another classic tool. PEST analysis requires a rethink for relevance as well. PEST is a go-to for categorizing macro-level trends. The acronym stands for political, economic, socio-demographic, and technological. I'd been augmenting PEST with industry analysis to generate a wider view. You realize PEST is out-of-date when you consider:

+ Global issues such as population migration due to war or famine
+ Distorting forces such as the COVID-19 pandemic with its sweeping economic, health, and societal effects
+ Environmental changes such as global warming

Additionally, PEST analysis isn't optimal to address the disruptions, displacements, and distortions we see across the environmental and global spheres, from the pandemic and economic crises to the climate crisis.

As you learned in chapters 1 and 2, customer confusion and competitor encroachment are significant to your organization's future. You do your organization a disservice when your process focuses on appeasing board members rather than addressing trends with the power to shape and drive your future. When you address sweeping trends such as multiculturalism, you're more likely to catalyze fresh ideas and build consensus to change, as we've seen in our case studies.

Understand Context from a Customer Mindset

Customer mindset points the way to a holistic framework with six categories expressive of today's realities and tomorrow's possibilities.

Your Context

+ **People**—embraces broad sweeping consumer trends, social trends, and sociodemographic shifts such as racial equity and urbanization, in addition to classics such as differences across generational cohorts
+ **Economy**—studies economic conditions, trends, and outlooks such as gentrification and urban-rural divides
+ **Environment**—looks at climate change, weather crises, natural disasters, and environmental risks
+ **Technology**—spots trends like the digital divide and rollouts of technologies such as virtual reality, artificial intelligence, and the Internet of Things
+ **Public Policy**—monitors political trends, public policies, and the business of government at local, state, and federal levels. Political polarization and population displacements due to political unrest and war exemplify these trends
+ **Global**—encompasses the sweep and scale of a force from city, state, or region, to national and global. For example, climate change has local, national, and international implications

Embrace a customer mindset as you group forces, trends, and conditions into these six categories, noting the sweep of each from local to global. You'll learn how in chapter 7.

Watch Out for the Rabbit Hole

Social media and the internet are perfect examples of twenty-first-century rabbit holes. The realization that ten or thirty minutes later, you may have been sidetracked by a passing fancy

> Your customer is the person whose life you promise to impact through mission delivery.

or whim of an idea is frustrating. How about, for example, when you were looking for a source on philanthropic giving but ended up on TMZ's website?

It's easy to get distracted by clickbait when analyzing your organization's external context. I refer to those tangents as rabbit holes. Many of the attention-grabbing topics don't bring clarity of understanding to current customer preferences or future competitor actions.

When you get caught up in the issue of the day, you're likely to miss the forces with the greatest influence. That compelling political story that captured your board member's imagination isn't likely to impact your customers. The widespread adoption of e-commerce, on the other hand, is a trend worth noting.

Recognize This Is Uncharted Territory for Strategists Driven by Purpose

Let's make another visit to the dean's desk. The perfect storm arrived in the form of the COVID-19 pandemic with sweeping implications for higher education. Overnight, classes were canceled and moved online as institutions navigated uncertainty, ambiguity, and volatility. Students graduated with yard signs and virtual ceremonies. Some wondered if attending next year online was worth the cost. This inflexible model bent by a distortion it could not withstand was about to come to a head.

The COVID-19 pandemic distorts; it isn't merely a disruption or displacement. Some of its consequences will alter daily life for years in unexpected ways. New habits are being formed; old rituals are being abandoned. The unorthodox is becoming standard as invention replaces proven. Watchwords to consider include rediscover, reimagine, and reinvent.

Strategists are experienced with economic downturns, increasing consumer expectations, and industry upheaval, certainly. But a pandemic? These are epochal times, given the virus's societal upheaval. Our ten-year journey of economic expansion fell off the cliff in a matter of weeks. This is new. You will be navigating these issues for several years at a minimum. This won't be one and done. You know what I'm going to say again—this is new. What remains the same is the need to understand the external context from your customer's mindset. The pandemic is prompting us to evaluate a holistic list of contextual considerations, including people, technology, politics and public policy, the economy, the environment, and global issues.

Your organization's future is defined by this suite of factors. They form the backdrop. They do not create the focus. That's up to you.

Your differentiation strategy is your chosen direction built from a thorough understanding of your customers, competitors, and context. In chapter 7, you'll learn more about how context, customers, and competitors come together in "Step One: Understand Your Customers, Competitors, and Context."

I leave you with a call to action. It's never been more important to differentiate your organization. Your ongoing success depends on your ability to clearly articulate distinction in the marketplace, craft a resilient strategy to advance it, enthrall donors and influencers to embrace it, engage with customers to achieve it, and demonstrate relevance through mission impact to sustain it.

Every organization won't make it through to the next normal. New entities will emerge and others will merge, be acquired, or close their doors. The landscape is forever altered by the COVID-19 pandemic.

ESSENTIAL LEARNINGS

Principle Four: Your Environment Creates Context, Not Focus

1. Goodbye SWOT and PEST. Hello context.
2. Understand context from a customer mindset.
3. Watch out for the rabbit holes.
4. Recognize this is uncharted territory for strategists driven by purpose.

5.

Principle Five: You Compete in More Than One Industry

Clear Your Cache

You heard the coos amid the claps and drumbeats. They sounded so happy. You couldn't help but walk toward them. You'd stopped by to check out the music classes. While you weren't "into babies," your feet propelled you down the corridor.

Then a peek through the window. Infants, maybe a year old, were sitting on the floor, each propped up by an adult. Women outnumbered men. The bongos were so small. Tiny hands clasped by loved ones moved up and down on the drums—pat, pat, pat—creating the beat. Toothless smiles preceded the laughter. Everyone paused. The smiles got even bigger. Then they clapped.

You turned back toward the entrance of Swallow Hill Music and the reception area. You'd been researching music classes online, fulfilling the promise you'd made to yourself to get back into music. Music had sustained you through high school and college. Somehow, you'd let it slip as your career began. You'd kept your banjo on display, hoping it would taunt you into taking it up again. Then a birthday gift of lessons.

You could engage in a class through a noted university or attend a music and yoga session. It seemed that everything went with yoga. The staff was persuasive in their pitch. You could sample a class anytime. Plus, your favorite musician was performing next month. But what about that retreat? Or the live-streamed course from South Carolina? That person was amazing and a bit of a recluse. You'd never see them in person, otherwise. There were so many good options to consider.

You stepped away from the Swallow Hill Music reception desk for a moment to soak it all in. Your banjo nodded yes. You'd brought it with you to experience how it felt to be with music again. The sensation moved up your fingers and arms to your heart. It was back. That same sense of joyful belonging you felt ten years ago. "I'd like to sign up for that class," you told the receptionist. A few steps and an Apple Pay swipe later, you were in. You'd found your home in music once again. At Swallow Hill Music.

Once you returned to your condo, you cleared the cache on your browser. No need to save the links to those online programs and out-of-state offerings. The recluse wasn't going anywhere.

Keywords Reveal a World of Possibilities

Experiences like this one illustrate the expanding array of options at your customer's fingertips. Each of us is a keyword away from pages of possibilities. Thanks to those terms and search engine optimization (SEO), it has never been easier to expand across industries. Isn't that a powerful realization?

A keyword signifies what matters to your customer—what they want, who they are, and where they are going. If that customer matters to me, then there is little to prevent me from pursuing your customer. Look, you have a new alternative competitor or—gulp—a catapult.

You rely on word-of-mouth marketing, too. Your customer asks their friends and family for advice and recommendations, knowing they've done the research. Which brings us back to the power of keywords. Those selected terms allow your customer to categorize, sort, and prioritize

Your customer is the person whose life you promise to impact through mission delivery.

options. Then they discover "the one" as illustrated by my story about The Logan School parent and the banjo player at Swallow Hill Music.

As purpose-driven organizations adopt online offerings, social media, SEO, and target marketing, they will expand their reach across industry lines; the same holds true at for-profits. Nothing is stopping others from encroaching on your market if there is market share to be gained, mission to be delivered, and revenue to be earned.

Let's say you want to learn more about art. Online research and friendly referrals reveal that:

+ Colleges offer online courses in art history
+ History museums sell art books
+ Art historians market online streamed courses from their branded websites and teach at the museum and college
+ A community art school offers a webinar showcasing a specific artist's technique
+ An artist leads Facebook Live how-to courses on her novel technique
+ A retailer's app is a gateway to free demonstration classes

Google any of the examples above and see where the search takes you. You'll discover various price points, features, benefits, and brand promises. Look a bit further and you'll discover different industries and sectors are represented.

You can't rely on a sector to narrow your search for competitors. More businesses commit to social benefit outcomes. Government agencies rely on e-commerce to deliver the customer experience. Nonprofits are social enterprises. Now more than ever, the lines between sectors—nonprofit, government, and nonprofit—have blurred.

The same applies to industries. Chapter 3's take on competitors—replacements, alternatives, catapults, and community builders—underscores the reality. Industry boundaries no longer apply. What defines arts and culture today? What about recreation and entertainment? Did they cross the mind of our banjo player? Or did they type music lessons and banjo and wait to see what the world had to offer?

It's easier than ever to leap over traditional boundaries into new markets. Tax status and industry don't limit your possibilities. Say hello to the tipping point.

Industry Boundaries No Longer Apply

Your customer isn't bound by traditional industry definitions. There is a good chance they aren't thinking about industry at all. They focus on what matters to them. If they are looking for a fun family activity, they don't care if you are a museum, shopping mall, or city-run park. They do care about your hours, parking, family-focused activities, and if you offer something special. They'll be there in droves if their kiddos are happy. An organization that got its start in industry A serving market niche B can easily expand into your arena. The Logan School is well-versed in these competitive realities.

Thanks to disruptive technologies and platform-based business models, an increasing number of organizations span multiple industries. Companies like Amazon, Square, and Google bring new combinations, capabilities, and opportunities as they create new industries. The result? More mashups are created as old boundaries fall away; fusion is the new theme.

Look Beyond Your Comfort Zone

Imagine you are the CEO of Swallow Hill Music. The customer research you've conducted sheds new light on a broader array of industries that you would not have considered in the past. You have your banjo player to thank for broadening your perspective.

You set to work learning more about the trends and forces shaping these industries:

+ Wellness—yoga classes
+ Music education—online courses
+ Early childhood education—mommy-and-me programs
+ Entertainment—concerts
+ Performance venues—small theaters
+ Recreation—fun family activities

This path of discovery leads you to understand the drivers and shapers of customer choices and competitor actions. Chapter 4's lessons were reinforced through industry analysis. From there, you'll dig deeper to understand what matters most to your customer as you apply the lessons from chapter 1. You'll consider choice from your customer's perspective, such as:

+ What can I do for fun?
+ What provides an escape from the everyday?
+ What can I enjoy with my family?
+ What aids the development of my child?
+ What satisfies my need for a home away from home? A place where I belong?
+ What's convenient?
+ What fits my budget?

It's clear now. Your view would have been restricted if you'd only studied nonprofit folk music performance venues. That's a specific niche market.

You can gain so much when you consider the factors influencing related and unrelated industries as they overlap with your market. Your customers and competitors aren't limiting themselves with narrow definitions of sector, industry, or mission. You shouldn't either. Just ask Hollywood as it competes with TikTok, Hulu, Amazon, and more.

Let's summarize the learnings from this chapter. The lines delineating industries and sectors have blurred to the point of irrelevance, freeing you to consider myriad fields in which you compete—the tried and true and new ones. Cataloging the array of competitors aids you in uncovering the other industries you compete in. You can learn so much from their strategic moves. Don't miss the "aha" moment here, as it has tremendous potential for your future strategy. You can extend your mission impact into other industries, too. Once again, customer mindset points the way to fresh thinking.

Let's ready ourselves for the Differentiation Zone's final principle, which is explained in "Principle Six: Watch Out for the Zone of Indifference." While "Principle One: It's All About the Customer" centers us in what matters to our customers, "Principle Six: Watch Out for the Zone of Indifference" shines a bright light on what doesn't matter to our customers. If you look closely, you can see them shrugging instead of smiling.

ESSENTIAL LEARNINGS

Principle Five: You Compete in More Than One Industry
1. Keywords display a world of possibilities.
2. Industry boundaries no longer apply.
3. Look beyond your comfort zone.

6.

Principle Six: Watch Out for the Zone of Indifference

Not So Much

You recall the experience as if it were yesterday. You took a breath, put on your smile, and walked across the room. "Hi, it's wonderful to meet you."

You got carried away talking about the founder's legacy. After all, you'd only been CEO for less than a month. It was such an honor to take up where your predecessor left off. Your organization followed the typical startup journey replete with sweat equity, sacrifice, and the special pride of survivalists. You've heard the stories. The folklore and myths convey the early culture. The old building and its summertime suffering; no money for air conditioning. A muumuu would have to do. Some got by with shorts. Then the revolt against yoga pants. The call for a dress code came next. The up and down cycles of customers, money, and morale. Your organization was flourishing, having survived it all. It wasn't easy being a nonprofit. Where did all this new competition come from?

You felt compelled to speak about the incoming board chair with your guest. The chair's tenure as finance chair, then fundraising co-chair, prepared them to lead your organization during turbulent times. Thank goodness they'd led the organization through the 2008 economic crisis. They made sure you had a small reserve now. That took some work.

Your guest grinned. But you noticed their eyes flit about, a sure sign they weren't interested in your founder or board chair. Then they pulled out their phone, pretending to have an important text. Once the phone was stowed away, you weighed the options of mentioning your investment in new software or that your staff turnover was below the industry standard. What about the outcomes data? Everyone loved hearing about the numbers. Where was that graph?

You knew your prospective customer was interested in how your organization was expanding mission impact to serve a family and community like theirs—diverse, growing, and engaged. They were hungry for opportunities. Your city had changed remarkably over the last two years. Households embodied new definitions of what it meant to be a family, some preferring to identify with a family of choice instead of a family of origin. They also wanted to know what you were doing to close the gap—the learning gap, the achievement gap, and the opportunity gap. Maybe you'd offer your go-to quip: "Mind the gap," as they say in the United Kingdom.

You paused. They spoke. The rapid-fire questions signaled what mattered most after all. Could you share stories of families and kids? What did they love about your programs? What features resonated most? Did you have any pictures or videos?

"Yes," you replied, with a big smile. "Let me show you our Instagram feed."

Those Features May Be Dear to You but Are Unimportant to Your Customer

The new CEO's inner dialogue that I've just described is a common occurrence in organizations driven by purpose. Passionate leaders meet with prospective customers and often miss the mark as they describe what they do rather than share stories of why they matter. It's so easy to let our passion overtake the narrative. Rather than making our customer the hero of the story, we focus on our own accomplishments. In this case, the CEO was fortunate that the prospect began to ask questions, offering cues about their interests.

Keeping the CEO's misfire in mind, let's dust off an essential learning from chapter 1. You want to matter most to the people who matter most to you—your customers. That realization is the source of your organization's differentiation strategy. You begin by understanding what is important to your customer and what is not. We call the "doesn't matter" category the Zone of Indifference. Your customer may love your intuitive website, while your volunteer retention strategy may not be important to them. A friendly person helping your child learn something new may matter most of all.

> Your customer is the person whose life you promise to impact through mission delivery.

Indifference is a signal, an indicator that your feature is unimportant, meaningless, or irrelevant to your customer. Consequently, your customer may be apathetic or disinterested in it. I know that might sound harsh, but let's face it—they aren't into the same stuff as you.

Take a minute to reflect on the language. When I speak about what matters to your customer, I use the terms feature, benefit, and attribute—language that is customer-centric. In contrast, I do not use the words capacity or capability. Those terms are organization-facing. They describe your organization's functions, not the elements of high value to your customer. It may help to think of it this way: capabilities are the means; benefits are the ends.

Your Zone of Indifference is home to elements such as organizational history and legacy, board leadership and structure, customer management software, staff tenure, and customer-facing features and attributes that no longer resonate.

Strategy is directional. The act of direction setting requires a scan of the external landscape, the shapers and drivers of opportunities. Looking outside isn't optional; it's crucial.

Internal Capabilities Are Not Strategic Differentiators

You take pride in your organization. Your staff, board, and volunteers spend countless hours enhancing capabilities, improving websites, deciphering data, perfecting events, and tracking revenues, goals, and deadlines. That matters, doesn't it? Your confusion about customers and your tendency to think of all stakeholders as customers pushes you into the Zone of Indifference without realizing you've gone from "Oh, wow!" to "Not so much."

We discover indifference when we listen to understand. In our CEO's case, the list of unimportant items might have included the origin story and the folklore beloved by long-tenured staff. The same holds true for the board chair's background and the financial reserve. Observation reveals so much.

Here's a trick: emphasize the core of your mission. In this example, our CEO leads an upskilling center with a proven ability to close the opportunity gap. Its customers rave about personal fulfillment and pride of accomplishment. Customers participate on their own terms via cell phone, online chatting, and tutorials, which means they succeeded. They graduate and compete successfully for jobs. Laid-off waiters discover they can get smart on coding thanks to the course offerings. But you didn't hear any of this reflected in our CEO's internal dialogue.

Brace yourself. Your board and staff may pout a bit when you move beloved items from this list into the Zone of Indifference during Step Three of your process. I've seen those same dismissive looks before. Yes, they matter to you. No, they don't matter to your customer.

Begin by distinguishing between organizational capabilities and customer-facing attributes. The former won't lead to differentiation, while the latter is essential to name and claim it. Get ready for a bit of tough love. You have invested in customer-facing features that are no longer important to your customer. That is an issue of market relevance essential to consider for differentiation.

Now, I'm sure you are nodding in agreement.

Watch out for the Zone of Indifference. Don't let your passion for the organization keep you from reading what your customers care about, as our fictional CEO did in this chapter scenario. That's a sign you're thinking your organization is the declarative I. Let go of that habit. As was discussed in the introduction, we aren't concerned with your capabilities.

Join me in saying goodbye to the Zone of Indifference. Your customers don't value some of the features you hold dear. Focus on what your customer values. Set those features aside so you can focus on your Differentiation Zone.

ESSENTIAL LEARNINGS

Watch Out for the Zone of Indifference

1. Those features may be dear to you but are unimportant to your customer.
2. Internal capabilities are not strategic differentiators.

Section 2
The Essence of Your Strategy Is Choice

Welcome to My Studio

Back in the day, when we used to "watch television," there was a show called *The Actor's Studio*. It was captivating to observe actors speaking about mastering their craft as they recalled their roles and career-defining performances. Section 2 of this book is my version of that studio, as I share my craft with you.

My role as a facilitator defined the early years of my strategic planning career. I worked with the expertise of my client to determine the way forward. Often, during a retreat, someone like you would ask me to share an observation about the state of nonprofits, notable trends, and which organizations were doing something special. Over time, I stepped out more often with an opinion or two. Eventually, I opened each retreat by setting the stage with my point of view.

I spent the last ten years training my brain to be more astute at making connections and cognitive leaps. From there, I worked on formulating original insights. Hundreds of in-person meetings honed my ability to think on the fly. When ten, twenty, or thirty people are looking to you for direction and the answer, clear thinking and swift responses are essential for success.

The pathway to mastering my craft is manifested in self-identity. I evolved from calling myself a facilitator to referring to myself as a strategic planner. For several years I've made this proclamation: I am a strategist.

The evolution of my professional identity is linked to my journey as an artist. Painting found me, thanks to a Canvas and Cocktails event ten years ago. There I was, in a ballroom surrounded by forty other would-be artists for an evening of wine-inspired team building the night before the annual retreat. My field of aspens looked a bit like everyone else's and altogether different. It was a happy accident, as PBS artist Bob Ross would say. An unplanned event with beneficial outcomes and, for me, pleasant surprises. Within a week, I purchased painting supplies.

From an Unknown World to Breaking New Ground

"Art is an adventure into an unknown world, which can be explored only by those willing to take risks," wrote artists Mark Rothko and Adolph Gottlieb in a letter to the *New York Times*. My comfort with the unknown expanded with my tolerance for risk. Art was my activator, like yeast is to bread.

Every artist learns to recognize when a piece is complete. There is always the possibility that one additional mark may diminish—or worse—ruin a piece. The act of standing in front of a canvas, knowing that a painting was complete, no other stroke or mark required, taught me to recognize when my strategic creations were complete, as well.

My strategy insights came together in two lessons. Section 1 introduced you to one lesson through the Six Guiding Principles. It's time to embrace your customer's mindset. I've boiled my ten thousand hours of strategy experience into a second lesson—the essence of your strategy is choice. As you read in the introduction, strategy is directional. Too many strategic plans fail because they aren't strategic at all. There is no chosen direction. They don't say no to say yes.

Section 2's lesson is all about getting you to yes. More specifically, my goal is to show you how to select the most precise yes of all—a differentiation strategy rooted in customer mindset bonded to mission and success measures.

Achieving the second lesson's full potential for your organization requires mastery of the first. In case you are tempted to bail now, let me outline the consequences of using an out-of-date strategy model. Many tools expired a few years back or, as you've read, several decades ago. They didn't adjust to the realities of the customer zeitgeist. The world tipped forward and left them behind.

There are several notable hidden costs when you use models that do not recognize the seismic shift in customer mindset. By now, you are familiar with the effects of tools such as SWOT and PEST as we discussed in chapter 4. From one strategist to another, I'd avoid these risks:

+ Being left behind as your competitors adapt to changing customer preferences
+ Undervaluing your customer's power to determine the rules of engagement with your organization
+ Underestimating the threat of new entrants to your market due to replacements, catapults, and community builders vying to matter more to your customers
+ Overestimating your organization's ability to navigate complex and quick changes such as societal, environmental, and public health crises

Get ready to experience your Differentiation Zone process step by step as you put to work the Six Guiding Principles. Bring your essential learnings with you. Along the way, I'll introduce you to new approaches reflecting the latest thinking about customers, competitors, and context as well as the big reveal of your Differentiation Zone tool.

Principle One: It's All About the Customer.
Principle Two: Not Every Stakeholder Is a Customer.
Principle Three: Competition Is Prevalent.
Principle Four: Your Environment Creates Context, Not Focus.
Principle Five: You Compete in More Than One Industry.
Principle Six: Watch Out for the Zone of Indifference.

Let's meet your Four-Step Process.

Step One: Understand Your Customers, Competitors, and Context. Your journey begins with a disciplined study of your customers, competitors, and context. You gather research and take stock of your organization. Techniques to help you harmonize key data with trends such as shifts in the economy, society at large, public policy, technology, and consumer behavior come next.

Step Two: Reveal Customer and Competitor Insights. Now, you uncover original insights from data gathered and synthesized in the first step. Following a facilitated conversation, you complete this phase with an honest understanding of what matters most to your customers, what matters least, and what sets you apart in the marketplace.

Step Three: Discover Differentiation to Drive Strategic Success. Now you experience the signature step of the process. You "call the question" through a series of conversations to identify the essential elements that belong in your Differentiation Zone. You also shift what customers find unimportant to the Zone of Indifference. You conclude this step with a clear and powerful description of your organization's differentiators.

Step Four: Design Your Differentiation Zone Strategy. You've arrived. This is the design phase armed with everything you need to know about your customers, competitors, and context. Now you create your chosen strategy, using the differentiators declared in the previous step. A facilitated process leads you to build a plan. You make your strategy a reality and, if desired, optimize your business model.

The Right Tool in Hand

Differentiation Zone's Four-Step Process presents you with a creative opportunity of your own. As you prepare your studio, set aside your usual brush and reach for the tool you just acquired. Pick up the lesson from section 1—to embrace your customer's mindset—and take it in hand. Get comfortable with how it feels. Prepare to discipline yourself in using it, as I do. Still today. Every. Time.

> Your customer is the person whose life you promise to impact through mission delivery.

Notice you aren't creating a self-portrait. Rather, your mind's eye finds the one whose lived experience fills the portrait. Your customer is in sight. The Six Guiding Principles prepared you for this moment.

Up Next: Your Original Creation

There you are, standing in front of your fresh canvas, customer mindset in hand. The first mark made. Then, in a flash, the painting is complete. Your work of art is clearly differentiated.

7.

Step One: Understand Your Customers, Competitors, and Context

My Why

Hi. My friends call me J. Welcome to my audio blog. Here's a bit of background for new listeners. Much to my mom's dismay, I didn't go right to college after high school. My bridge year turned into four. I've been working the frontlines of hunger relief with a community-based nonprofit. For the past two years, I've been working on college campuses. I also have a side hustle building apps. A knack for programming helps pay the bills.

For this month's blog post, I thought I'd take you on a college tour. Let's start at the school of engineering and computer science. When I ask college students what they're studying, they tell me about data science, the Internet of Things, and virtual reality. Seems you can go anywhere with a degree in computer science, even to the moon or Mars with NASA. Across campus, I meet students exploring fields like epidemiology. Who knew public health could be so inspiring? I read that pandemics reveal health disparities and underlying social justice issues. Speaking of justice issues, I saw that the

United Nations identified a set of sustainable development goals for the planet, one of which is hunger. It's exciting to know that my work puts me in the center of a global challenge.

I have a big announcement this month. I'm ready for college. I have a list of must-haves, like hands-on problem-solving and teamwork. Plus, I want inspiring faculty and interesting courses that can open doors for me. I also want to lead a team project or two. Ultimately, I want to have a career in public service and hold a master's in public policy or law. Then I'd like to run for office. We need to change some laws if we're going to make a dent in these global challenges.

I've narrowed my undergraduate options to computer science, international affairs, and public health. Each field addresses big problems and involves creativity. And skills like mine are needed. Coding is considered the new second language for twenty-first-century professionals. My timing couldn't be better.

So, the computer science dean has taken an interest in me. I've read that access and inclusion are really important in the computer science field. Without it, there's the potential to embed bias in computer code, which could affect the algorithms that run our lives. Oh, I better text yes to that invitation. Look, here's one from the international affairs program. That dean likes me, too.

A Note From Your Strategy Coach

By design, this opening story is told from the first-person point of view from your customer's perspective. That creative device was essential to illustrating the importance of customer mindset when analyzing your customers, competitors, and context. Imagine if we led with the traditional approach. The dean would have served as your narrator, sharing a story about the prospective student. A dean may emphasize new program offerings in high-demand fields rather than highlight the must-have list. A dean certainly wouldn't have known about the range of competitors at hand. The dean would have spoken about the prospective student in a third-person perspective, diminishing the customer's power. The same happens when you narrate your customer's story. You interpret their why. You get caught up in what you do, forgetting why you matter.

I'm not inviting you to try on customer mindset. I'm asking you to wholeheartedly embrace it. You aren't giving a nod to the voice of the customer. You become the customer from this page forward. The more adept you are at viewing choice from your customer's perspective, the more successful you'll be with this process. Without that habit of mind, you won't discover your organization's Differentiation Zone.

Your customer owns the story, just as our blogger owns this story. Their why is the one that matters. The Logan School cemented the importance of customer mindset for me. Now it's your turn. Your customer becomes the declarative I.

My Why, Redux

Let's join our food security champion in accepting the dean's invitation. Imagine you and I are prospective students listening to the pitch and mingling with faculty and current students. We hear stories of meaningful careers and pathways to a sought-after life of community service. Can you envision yourself achieving your must-haves? Are you feeling a special connection? Do they grasp what matters most to you?

This look into the prospective student's decision-making experience brings customer mindset to life, combining the essential learnings from the Six Guiding Principles. You already know the student's parents aren't your customer, tempted though you may be, given their alumni status and fundraising potential. Chapter 2 drove that lesson home. Repeat after me: "Not every stakeholder is a customer." You've also glimpsed the hyper-dynamic environment surrounding higher education in chapter 4.

Principle One: It's All About the Customer.
Principle Two: Not Every Stakeholder Is a Customer.
Principle Three: Competition Is Prevalent.
Principle Four: Your Environment Creates Context, Not Focus.
Principle Five: You Compete in More Than One Industry.
Principle Six: Watch Out for the Zone of Indifference.

A Wicked Problem

Higher education is a powerful learning lab for strategists that's chock-full of unexpected competitor moves and changing customer expectations operating in a dynamic context. Let's look more closely at this setting and consider a school of engineering and computer science, for example.

A new dean walks into this academic world, fresh from industry. The engineers and computer scientists face a wicked problem they can't readily solve—the persistent lack of diversity in their classrooms and professions. The world needs more engineers and computer scientists. Millions of unfilled jobs are a testament to the reality. Research shows that diverse teams deliver better results. Their solutions are more creative, and companies with diverse cohorts outperform rivals. If the school can't attract diverse students to these professions, they will miss opportunities to accelerate success for companies and communities worldwide.

If the fields aren't attractive, then the school won't be competitive. It isn't merely a matter of going toe-to-toe with other computer science programs, for example. The strategic stakes are much higher. You don't need an engineering or computer science degree to address sticky problems. Engineering and computer science aren't just vying with science and math; they are contending with other disciplines such as international affairs and social science, as our blogger pointed out.

A radical reframing is in order. Thousands of future space explorers, sustainable energy innovators, and food security disruptors are waiting in the wings. Prospective students determine if the school is relevant or not. The spotlight shines most brightly on those historically underrepresented— students of color and women.

Customer Mindset Points to Your Solution

Our focus in Step One is understanding the deep empathy-based and data-driven appreciation essential to discovering differentiation in the marketplace. Stories from The Logan School and the Children's Museum of Denver at Marsico Campus give you a sense of the insights we seek. So does the narrative of our prospective student.

Join me, the dean, and faculty as we fashion new conduits to strategic insights. We'll introduce you to your new toolkit. We'll also let go of old standby tools created before the tipping point. SWOT and PEST aren't up to the task at hand, as we explored in section 1.

Meet your new go-to framework. Your goal is to realize what motivates customer choice and drives competitor action. My advice—be the customer.

Step One: Understand Your Customers, Competitors, and Context.
Step Two: Reveal Customer and Competitor Insights.
Step Three: Discover Differentiation to Drive Strategic Success.
Step Four: Design Your Differentiation Zone Strategy.

Your Three Cs: Customers, Competitors, and Context

Arriving at an understanding in Step One builds from a thorough analysis of your customers, competitors, and context—your Three Cs. To better recognize higher education's strategic issues, let's zero-in on the customer-centered realities faced by the dean and faculty.

Understanding Your Customers

Chapter 1 taught you the two reasons to be crystal clear about your customers: they decide what matters to them, and they define the competitive set that matters to you. This is all the more reason to begin by clarifying your customer.

> Your customer is the person whose life you promise to impact through mission delivery.

Let's explore an example. A purpose-driven young adult with coding skills has a far-ranging set of options to consider beyond the traditional routes of engineering and computer science. At the core, they are drawn to careers filled with problem-solving, creative thinking, and solutions generating. Courses and degrees aren't the only significant factors they consider. They also think about extracurricular activities, electives, dual degrees, and the extent to which students can design their educational experience, much like we saw at The Logan School. They seek high ROI, given the realities of student loan debt.

Grounding yourself in mission is the first step in clarifying your customer. Focus on the person whose life you promise to impact through mission delivery. We also know from chapter 2 how important it is to delineate your customer from stakeholders. Honor your stakeholders as you set them aside for now.

This mindset shines a powerful spotlight on your customers, including those you haven't served well or at all, as we've appreciated in this story. Historically underrepresented communities claim their rightful place in your mission and your strategy; they aren't simply relegated to diversity initiatives. Their expectations, aspirations, and unmet needs are in full view as you create personas.

Customer Personas Tell the Story

Personas are multifaceted portraits of your customers. Recall that our definition of customer mindset is the holistic view of your customer, recognizing head and heart. Customer mindset defines your personas, too, just as you began to see with the prospective student.

Personas aid in clarifying facts and testing assumptions. I encourage you to craft persona profiles for each of your customer groups. Describe who they are, what they care about (and don't), and how they engage with your purpose-driven organization. Create sketches of your customers as people. Who are they? What are they like? What matters? What matters most? Use psychographic data to frame their personality. Then use demographics to add dimension.

You may determine that your organization has two, three, or perhaps four personas inclusive of all customers. The dean would discover the school had four personas—the traditional engineering student, the traditional computer science student, and under-represented students in each profession. Understanding what matters most to future engineers and computer scientists is essential to attracting diverse talent, backgrounds, cultures, and capabilities.

Your goal is to envision your customer as a whole person and appreciate their individual agency, as we learned with the children's museum in chapter 1. Don't forget the expectations of people who do not engage with your organization as much as you'd like. The choice is theirs, as are their desires and expectations. Your task is to understand what drives their choices and actions. You'll also begin to see what doesn't matter. These are details you'll need later for the Zone of Indifference in chapter 9.

Your colleagues in marketing and branding are likely aware of personas because this technique is often used in their work. You may invite them to assist you in creating personas to guide your organization's differentiation strategy. They probably have data you can use as well, including your admissions, membership, alumni, advancement, enrollment, and program offices.

Let's join the dean's team in creating personas for the undergraduate program of the Ritchie School of Engineering and Computer Science. They know that the generation entering college cared deeply about impact. Their K-12 education was rich with community service projects and team learning experiences. Prospective students grasped key data points about deforestation in the Amazon as quickly as they digested air quality issues in American cities. They knew the customer zeitgeist inside and out. After all, they grew up with it.

This generation demands transparency and seeks to make a difference during their college years, and they aren't going to wait. Appealing to them, especially to individuals historically underrepresented in these fields, requires a change in perspective. The language, images, and metaphors that appeal to the classic persona attracted to engineering and computer science have less draw for the people who didn't see themselves or their communities in those stories. They have their own stories—and those stories matter. If a prospective student can't see themselves within these programs, they'll find what they seek someplace else.

I hope it's ingrained in your memory now, after all these pages with me. Your customer defines your competitive set. Personas provide a glimpse into your customer's other options, and that knowledge will inspire you to learn more about the competition.

Understanding Your Competitors

Let's join the dean and faculty in a real or virtual conference room. We are wrapping our collective minds around the new nature of competition.

Customer research reflects the challenge at hand: the school competes in more than one industry, which we discussed in chapter 5. We used to think of ourselves as solely competing with other engineering and computer science programs to pursue higher rankings and other traditional markers of success. We believed they were the primary characteristics driving customer choice when they are, in fact, part of the equation. Those traditional measures define the competitive set from the school's perspective. Customer mindset points to the shift.

What if the prospective student cares more about career satisfaction, community impact, and work-life balance than a degree or field of study? Their interests are rooted in civic action and policy change. You already know the dean's prospect can be found on the cultivation list for the international affairs program, and likely others, too. Talk about unexpected competitors. Each of those fields is in search of students with creative problem-solving skills and a penchant for leadership. Recall, too, that supply exceeds demand in higher education. Colleges and universities are vying for market share, as we read in chapter 4.

Essential learnings about customers tie everything together. Your organization's mission and strategic relevance are centered on customer clarity, which is all the more reason for you to rally your internal experts and data sources to determine what additional research may be required. It's time to learn more about the unexpected alternatives your customers are considering, many of which are unknown to you.

Welcome to the World of Replacements, Alternatives, Catapults, and Community Builders

Say goodbye to direct, indirect, and substitute competitors. Open your mind to the world of replacements, alternatives, catapults, and community builders. They jump over industry boundaries in search of market share and profit margin. We'll join the dean's gathering to make sense of it all.

The prospective student's decision point serves as our living case study. Attuned to the latest options, with direct-to-consumer advertisements from other degree programs following their every move online, our prospect is well-versed in choice. Networks of friends and online groups share real-time news, and everyone is attuned to local, national, and global opportunities. The customer zeitgeist is in full force.

Expectations for personalization amplify the strategic imperative. "What's in it for me?" becomes "Why you?" The competition is inescapable and comes with unending comparison on demand.

Replacements

Your offering is categorized as a replacement when your customer views your product or service as easily replaceable by something similar. They may not be able to tell the difference between your offerings and others, leaving them feeling a bit confused or complacent. A confused customer may stick with what they know, as we see with the tendency to re-watch episodes of "Friends" rather than try something new. In this case, a parent's alma mater is the low-risk solution to your prospective student's problem.

Replacements are readily available from traditional rivals and those seeking a toehold in your market. Their products and services fill customer needs in a similar way. Replacements often rely on the brand to differentiate otherwise equivalent offerings. Regrettably, that is a shallow victory because a brand can be mimicked by competitors. If your educational experience can be matched by a community college or state college for half the cost or less, for example, the competitive power of replacements cannot be ignored.

The dean and faculty were well-versed in the traditional replacements in their fields. They recognized which entities offered comparable educational experiences and which delivered more. The ante was upped often as programs across the globe fought to capture market share. The war for talent was fierce because the demand for graduates exceeded the supply.

Alternatives

Keywords reveal a world of possibilities. The prospective student can't help exploring alternative program designs, course requirements, and unusual combinations. Everything of interest is within reach online, and much of it comes to our prospective student without much effort, from boot camps and specialty programs to online courses and trade schools.

As your customers evaluate options, they are drawn to alternatives that meet their needs in unique ways. They may not have realized they wanted XYZ until they discovered it was available and designed just for them. There are exciting and unexpected ways to build the future, and you don't need a computer science degree to make a difference.

Alternatives present innovative designs and novel solutions. In higher education that may mean an unexpected degree, minor, or internship. What else could be possible if leadership is the focus? International affairs and public health, certainly. Alternatives offer something initially novel that eventually becomes readily available and ultimately a standard. There is little to prevent others from expanding into potential growth markets, some from entirely different industries. Our case studies in higher education and the arts exemplify this reality.

Don't forget, your customers are being wooed by traditional and unexpected competitors every day. They may be unfamiliar to you, but not to your customer. Direct-to-consumer marketing is the alternative's domain. Your customers are likely to learn of alternatives through marketing based on interest patterns. Their social media feeds will be filled with sponsored advertisements and opportunities to purchase.

Yesterday's alternative is today's replacement. Experiential education is a case in point. It used to be novel but now is deemed essential. Coding schools and other hands-on programs are alternatives to traditional undergraduate offerings. Hello, alternative credential. What can I do in one year instead of four?

Catapults

What matters most to your customer just landed in their lap, courtesy of a smartphone. Catapults meet customer needs in new and unprecedented ways through previously unavailable or unbelievable options. Catapults are a new possibility. They reinvent the features, benefits, and characteristics of products and services to address what matters most, bringing novelty to the market. Maintaining that edge isn't a foregone conclusion. Yesterday's novelty is today's alternative and on the path to replacement.

The prospective student just learned about a new program combining leadership, computer-based problem-solving, and direct community impact. It can be completed in two years for a fraction of the cost of a computer science degree.

When customers seek customization, convenience, and novelty, the possibilities of a catapult are increasingly likely, especially if they can be delivered at scale through a platform-based model. Unexpected strategic partnerships bring together necessary assets and core competencies. Imagine the possibilities if Google offered alternatives to traditional degree programs in high-demand technology fields. Scalable solutions to the sustainable development goals of the United Nations may be closer at hand, thanks to artificial intelligence and other technologies.

Community Builders

We yearn for connections and positive human interactions, especially in times of increasing anxiety and disagreement. A sense of community fulfillment expands the user experience. What matters most includes a heart connection in addition to a head-based logical solution. As your customers seek to address what matters most to them, they may consider possibilities to join communities.

For example, we know the prospective student is drawn to community-building leadership opportunities. Those may be found on a smaller campus deeply committed to project work with the local community where the student can create real-time solutions to wicked problems. Their differentiators? A novel evidence-based approach with lasting results. Community is in their DNA. Our prospective student is attracted to the possibilities of living in the community for years to come.

There is room for novelty here. Don't assume that yesterday's differentiators will meet today's demands for a one-of-a-kind experience. Committed to impact, educational organizations find meaningful ways to deliver on mission, often engaging in advocacy and awareness-raising. Community builders include registered B Corporations and other sector-spanning corporate forms. Who knows what novel approaches could appear to satisfy customer cravings for learning, impact, and community to achieve high ROI for less time and expense? A pandemic inspires creative solutions when an industry is being upended as we're seeing in higher education.

It's a Whole New World

Customer mindset leads to a more insightful understanding of who is vying to meet your customer's needs, whether you consider them competition or not. Now you have a more complete view of your competitors than if you'd applied the classic categories of direct, indirect, and substitute.

Framing your competitors as replacements, alternatives, catapults, and community builders extends the power of customer personas to your competitive analysis and allows you to describe competitors as well as industry dynamics and market forces most likely to drive competitor actions and influence customer decisions. For example, once you understand who is moving in as a catapult or community builder, you can reverse engineer to discover their industry and the other markets they serve. Soon you'll grasp the full mix of competitors that matter most to your customers.

Next, it's time to come to grips with where your competitors have a unique edge, where all of you are essentially equivalent, and where you may have a unique differentiator of strategic significance. You'll complete that task in chapter 8 when we explore customer and competitor insights.

Understanding Your Context

The swirl of change across higher education is gaining momentum, as you read in chapter 4, ranging from community expectations for civic leadership to student concerns with social justice, student loan debt, and ROI.

As we've learned alongside the dean and faculty, your customers and competitors are influenced by a range of forces, including societal trends, technological advances, political shifts, and economic cycles. Your competitors also are affected by changes in industries. You want to zero-in on the forces with the greatest potential to inform customer choice and drive competitor behavior. The prospective student is driven by a desire to make an immediate impact. The same holds true for their future classmates. The dean and faculty would be wise to recognize that expectation.

Your environment creates context, not focus. Let go of SWOT and PEST analysis tools since both reinforce dated thinking, particularly the notion that your organization is the declarative I. Customer mindset positions you to evaluate forces based on their potential to drive or shape actions.

Look for Shapers and Drivers

No, I'm not talking Spanx or Uber. As our explorations in the previous chapters have pointed out, our customers decide what matters most to them. Our task is to understand them. Your competitors are trying to decipher the same signals. As our case studies reveal, sweeping consumer expectations, economic conditions, and disrupting technologies have been major drivers over the past decade.

You can expect moves into your arena from unknown players, some with offerings unimaginable a short time ago. Insight-spotting taught me to fix my sights on the three to five forces with the greatest potential to shape your organization's future direction. These may include the trends, conditions, and forces affecting people, the economy, the environment, technology, public policy and, as long as it is a notable driving force, COVID-19. Don't forget to consider other industries where you compete. Chapter 5's lessons will be helpful in widening your view. I use questions like these to help me sift, sort, and prioritize.

+ How could ABC drive the preferences, choices, or actions
  of my customers?
+ How could XYZ influence the preferences, choices, or actions
  of my competitors?

Like the dean, your task is to determine which forces have the most profound impact now and are likely to shape your organization's future. That curated set of trends is the context for your strategy setting in chapter 9.

Embrace your customer's mindset as you group forces, trends, and conditions, noting the sweep of each from local to global. Then, zero in on the forces with the greatest potential to drive decisions and influence behaviors. That's where you should invest your time. These are the shapers and drivers.

If you make the mistake of skipping over this step, you'll find yourself immersed in an interesting but tangential debate with the potential to derail your process. Welcome to the dreaded rabbit hole accompanied by SWOT and PEST. I wouldn't stay down there too long if I were you.

Understanding Your Organization

Your final task in "Step One: Understand Your Customers, Competitors, and Context" is to take an honest look at your organization. I call it a tough-love assessment. This is the time to determine where your organization is exceptional and where it is simply ordinary. Those insights are crucial to determining differentiation.

For example, you may find that your organization is exceptional at converting customer data into product improvements ready for market in three months. Excellence attracts and retains customers at a rate far above industry standard. Conversely, you may determine that your online customer engagement portal is fairly ordinary. You are keeping up with industry standards, but you aren't setting the pace.

Tough Love It Is

Get ready to take stock of your organization's assets and limitations across customer-facing capabilities and internal capacities. You'll take a look at outcomes, engagement, marketing, financial management, and more. Recall from chapter 6 that your internal capabilities are not strategic differentiators. You cannot build a strategy around them, nor can you assume they are important to your customer. You know what to do—move them into the Zone of Indifference.

The findings from this task align with insights gleaned about your customer and what matters to them. You are on your way to answering two questions:

+ What matters to your customers, and what does not?
+ What distinguishes your organization from the competition?

Attunement and Alignment

I hope you are beginning to experience the power of customer mindset. Attunement with your customer begins with "Step One: Understand Your Customers, Competitors, and Context," which is informed by the Six Guiding Principles. Everything we've learned together is applied here in real time. You are defining the essential strategic issues for your organization. Alignment with your team starts now, too.

Here's what experience has taught me: if consensus is important to your culture and vital to your decision-making process, and if your organization and its context are complex, then you will need to invest more time and energy in this step. Why? Achieving consensus requires a standard baseline of empathy-based and data-driven information that all can read, study, and absorb. Your board and staff will grapple with customers, competitors, and context. You'll experience dialogue and debate, furrowed brows, nods, and wow moments. Your team needs time to process as they figure out what it all means, compare insights, and work to consensus-based conclusions. Recognize, too, that they are coming to terms with the reality that they are not your customer. Their diverse backgrounds and thinking styles are processing new ways of thinking about customers, stakeholders, and competitors. "Ah, I get it" and "Yes, that makes sense" are your aims.

I can begin to envision the long-awaited Differentiation Zone in "Step Three: Discover Differentiation to Drive Strategic Success." Your organization's future is worth the effort as you'll see in chapters 8 and 9. Empathy and data come together to reveal true insights that make you sit up and take notice. Make sure to bring an awareness of customer mindset with you and bookmark your Three Cs and tough-love assessment. Your synthesis muscle will get a good workout in "Step Two: Reveal Customer and Competitor Insights."

Of note as we close out this chapter, your strategy process is the perfect time to rethink your organization's mission as we discussed in chapter 1. Your analysis of context highlights untapped potential to fulfill your promise of mission impact in the future. We'll touch on relevance in chapter 10 when we set strategy. Alignment is in sight.

8.

Step Two: Reveal Customer and Competitor Insights

Kazoos and Business Suits

The Little Swallows eagerly line up on the outer wall of the ballroom while trying their best to keep quiet and not bunch together. The awards banquet was approaching its zenith as thirty or so kindergarteners and a handful of teachers stand in the stage wings. The little ones beam with big grins. Oh, it's time. The stage awaits. Here come the Little Swallows. Up they march. Then they form two rows. Could their grins be any bigger? A teacher moves to the front and positions herself. A verse. A rhyme. A song. Music is brought to life with such joy. The exuberance is indisputable. Clapping. Little bows. And then the quick march off the stage. What a treat.

With a hearty dose of eagerness that could only be matched by a children's performance, people in business attire gather at a luncheon for eight hundred. They pick up a whimsical instrument and perform an impromptu kazoo concert. Hum. Everyone dutifully follows the prompts with blowing and tooting. Wow, they're actually performing a song. This is fun. The experience is infectious. Surprise and delight ensue. Applause and smiles, too.

Joy can be loud or quiet. It might make you smile, laugh, or cry. It is always personal. Never given or granted. The experience is individual and sometimes collective. The agency is yours and mine. Each of us represents the declarative I.

> **Why does your organization matter?**
> **Why should it matter to me?**

A customer may say: *Because you make me feel.* For a few minutes or hours, you engage me in a memorable experience. I receive your invitation and readily accept. I hear notes, chords, words. Each element comes together in songs; the voices reflect the underlying meaning. I'm swept up, bowled over, teared up, and shut up by it all. Now I'm strumming, chording, learning, blowing, and humming. Experiencing myself as creator.

I feel alive. Instrument in hand. Song on my lips. And that's a gift.

From Offshoot to Joy Generator

For more than forty years, Swallow Hill Music had done its thing. That thing is folk music. Banjos were their specialty. The story goes that Swallow Hill Music came about as a venue for concerts and a space for music lessons, an offshoot of a folklore center down the street. It was the 1970s. You'll remember I took you on a brief tour in chapter 6 when you learned about the Zone of Indifference. I was the one with the banjo. The space is a bit funky now, showing its age. It's an acquired taste, much like the music, in a time of flash, fresh, chrome, and marble.

Customer mindset marks a detour in their forty-year journey. The early conversations and varied expressions of Swallow Hill Music's purpose were a telltale sign. Staff and board members talked about their mission on the stage and in the classroom. They staged concerts and held music classes onsite and at other venues. Their "petting zoo" of traveling instruments met kids in classrooms across the community. Musicians and teachers were the declarative I. What about the customer? They weren't really in the story at all, as if what mattered most weren't the people.

No wonder the new CEO couldn't share the why when we first met to talk about plans. The organization's language wasn't customer centered. More challenging still, its music genre felt detached for so many. What was all the rage in the 1960s and 1970s was much less so now. It left me wondering why Swallow Hill Music was relevant to the community beyond the folk music enthusiast. Banjo lovers were all over Swallow Hill Music. What about everybody else?

The new CEO reached out with a dilemma. "I don't know how to talk about our why. I can talk about what we do, but I don't have the language for why we matter." That was followed by, "I need the why to make a bigger impact through strategic growth, and to do that we need to expand our fundraising capabilities." The organization had strength in earned income and untapped potential in philanthropy. As you and I know, fundraising is nearly impossible without the why, especially when donors have the impression you don't need the money, earned income and all.

Competition was fierce and getting fiercer. New venues were opening, and festivals were springing up. More bands were performing. Music was everywhere, sure signs the city's and state's commitment to the art form was gaining traction. Music lovers were awash with options in person and online.

The CEO, board, and staff knew what they needed to do—showcase what made Swallow Hill Music special and, more importantly, demonstrate its distinct impact. Folk music has the power to connect and foster shared experiences, instilling a sense of community along the way. Kids and adults. Ukuleles and kazoos.

My antennae were up. I kept noodling over their challenge. As I did, I thought about the people whose lives Swallow Hill Music promised to impact through mission delivery. What about them? What's important to them? Whether that customer is a first grader benefiting from their school's free lunch program or a person of means buying season tickets to the concert series at the botanical gardens, at the core, they were people touched by music.

Remembering the Folk

Folk music is music of and for the people. Grounded in authenticity. Capturing the spirit of the time. Earthy. Genuine.

Somehow the people—the "folk" in folk music—were missing from Swallow Hill Music's mission and strategy. This wasn't to say that the staff and board weren't devoted to their work. Many had taken classes, some had taught them, and all enjoyed the concerts. Like many organizations driven by purpose, they got caught up in what they did, hoping that translated into why they mattered.

As we've learned, it's vital to focus on the people we serve and those we don't. The people who naturally gravitate to our mission and those we unintentionally leave out. We witnessed that disconnect between the museum and the engineering school. Swallow Hill Music faced the same challenge. Customer mindset's equity lens revealed it to us.

Let's join Swallow Hill Music for the second step of its Four-Step Process. We're picking up from the Three Cs discussed in chapter 7, "Customers, Competitors, and Context." After my noodling and the CEO's questioning, it was time to get clear about its customer. Customer personas paved the way.

+ Swallow Hill Folk: Folk music enthusiasts
+ Other Folk: People with the potential to be moved by folk music

---

Step One: Understand Your Customers, Competitors, and Context.
Step Two: Reveal Customer and Competitor Insights.
Step Three: Discover Differentiation to Drive Strategic Success.
Step Four: Design Your Differentiation Zone Strategy.

The first persona group embraced the organization's tried-and-true member—the concert goer, lesson taker, and teacher. They sought out Swallow Hill Music. The second persona encompassed everyone else, including the kids Swallow Hill Music served through school-based programs and other community members whose lives were enriched through musical experiences. They were the overlooked folk.

Our context analysis highlighted the trends and conditions influencing customer choices and driving competitor actions such as heightened awareness of equity, diversity, inclusion, and access; longer commute times; fewer quality musical programs in classrooms; an abundance of online and private lessons; and an increasing number of music venues throughout the metro area.

As we learned in chapter 7, personas invite us to dig deeply and understand our customers as whole persons—what drives them, motivates them, and engages them. Swallow Hill Music's task was to dig deeply enough to uncover similarities across personas—and differences, too. We wanted to identify its customers' shrugs and smiles.

Shrugs and Smiles

Emojis are a fun way to portray emotion. They summarize our state of being with a cartoon illustration. And they work beautifully when you are endeavoring to embrace your customer's mindset. Your task is to determine what matters to your customers. Recall my advice to be the customer. Does your offering make them shrug? Or will they smile? It's as simple as that.

Of course, Swallow Hill's folk may shrug less than other people. That's okay. We're really striving to understand what matters most—motivators, drivers, inspirers, and barriers.

Reveal What Matters Most to Your Customers

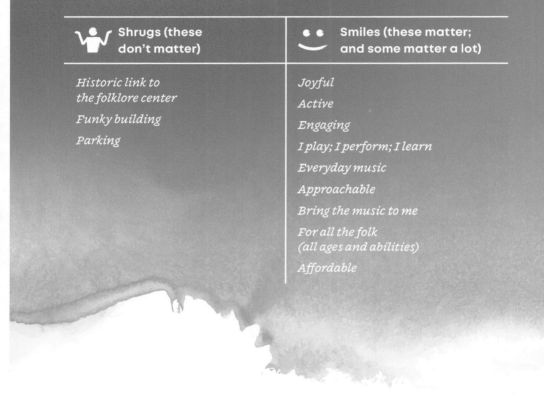

Shrugs (these don't matter)	Smiles (these matter; and some matter a lot)
Historic link to the folklore center	Joyful
Funky building	Active
Parking	Engaging
	I play; I perform; I learn
	Everyday music
	Approachable
	Bring the music to me
	For all the folk (all ages and abilities)
	Affordable

Your quest is differentiation—the uniquely compelling attributes, features, and benefits. Singularly you. That means you'll emphasize the items that matter most, with an ear toward what is exceptional and unique. You'll de-emphasize the not-so-much items that were top of mind in chapter 6. As you can see above, your customer is likely to be indifferent to internal capabilities that you hold dear, such as the historic link to the folklore center. Sorting them into the shrugs column is a precursor to placing them in the Zone of Indifference discussed in chapter 9.

To summarize, smiles include organizational features and attributes that are important, significant, relevant, and meaningful for customers. How do you know? Your customer told you.

Claiming Uniqueness

The next task was to see how Swallow Hill Music compares to the various musical offerings available to customers. Note, you'll want to ask your customers who else they may be considering because it will illuminate competitors you didn't know you had, as we learned in chapter 7. After you scan summaries of each competitor from "Step One: Understand Your Customers, Competitors, and Context," you'll sort the features, attributes, and benefits into three categories.

Reveal Uniqueness in the Marketplace

Unique to Competitors:
Proximity to growing neighborhoods

Not Unique to Any Organization:
Live music

Unique to Your Organization:
Folk music

Once again, we'll search your context for drivers and shapers. Focus on the forces with the greatest potential to shape Swallow Hill Music's future, such as the growth of the music market. There were more and more options on the stage and in the classroom. The city had an increasing appetite for live music. The city and region were becoming more diverse and international, too, with heightened expectations for cultural inclusion. Lastly, as families moved to outlying areas in search of affordable housing and quality schools, they sought offerings nearby. Who wanted to sit in traffic on the way to music class?

Competitors had an edge when it came to other music genres. They appealed to people who gravitated towards other forms and styles of music.

Some embodied cultural fluency and multiculturalism in ways that Swallow Hill Music did not. If other offerings were available and close-by, that was a plus too. If they were close in proximity and free, that was especially attractive.

What wasn't unique to any of the organizations, Swallow Hill Music included, was the availability of music on the stage or in the classroom. All the competitors offer one or both options. This is an "aha" moment because it confirmed Swallow Hill Music's prior framing wasn't distinctive or special. Also, many other competitors could claim the same quality standards in their respective genres.

Swallow Hill Music's ability to create joyful and meaningful musical connections through live folk music is unique. The Differentiation Zone approach led Swallow Hill Music to capitalize on this strength and recommit to the folk music genre in their mission.

Recentering on Purpose

Attunement and alignment reveal the essentials. "Step One: Understand Your Customers, Competitors, and Context" prepared you for the iterative work in "Step Two: Reveal Customer and Competitor Insights." Plan to facilitate a series of meetings to spark breakthroughs, reinforcing and exploring as you go. I hope you can envision the conversations, connections, and consensus-building involved. Our quest? Clarity with a customer mindset.

For me, it's a time to revisit Swallow Hill Music. I'm back in their funky building, facilitating a conversation with the board and staff and sharing my insight about the joy of folk music. Customer mindset placed me among my Little Swallow classmates who began this chapter and immersed me in a live musical experience. Folk music remembered all the folk.

We are gearing up for "Step Three: Discover Differentiation to Drive Strategic Success" of your Four-Step Process. You will discover the uniqueness that is singularly yours, the basis of your differentiation strategy. We can see Swallow Hill Music's differentiation emerging as it brings the joy of music to life every day. Insights reveal a singular essence at their core. The result? Mission, strategy, and outcomes aligned around their customer. Customer mindset revealed their differentiation.

9.

Step Three: Discover Differentiation to Drive Strategic Success

Welcome to the Wonder Dome

The laughter, mixed with chitchat, was almost deafening. Sixty staff members crowded around tables, some standing. An illustrator sat at each table, poised with markers in hand. Extra paper and sticky notes on call if needed. Their task: imagine the Children's Museum of Denver at Marsico Campus in 2040. Nothing was off-limits. They could be as bold and audacious as their hearts desired as long as they stayed true to the mission. Ready. Set. Go. The clock was ticking. Twenty minutes before show and tell.

Buzz. It was time for the big reveal. Who knew there were so many talented artists on staff? The drawings demonstrated all manner of enclosures, people movers, natural habitats, exhibits, and energy. Descriptive words were sprinkled across each drawing, declaring their hopes for kids and families. Everything imaginable was there under the wonder dome.

Play filled the dome and the conference room. Visions of kids zipping around, with their grown-ups in tow, came forth. Was that a paper airplane I saw overhead? Or a bubble?

But wait—we were early in the planning process. The visioning session was a time to hear what staff believed was possible. They were free to envision without constraints of time, money, popularity, or acceptability. The museum's play manifesto in hand.

The wonder dome became our icon, a visual symbol of collective aspirations. If 2040 was our aim, then a dome of wonder was surely possible—one with autonomous vehicles and others gliding in the air. Kids and grown-ups playing within its safe and happy confines. Exploring, imagining, learning, and creating.

And yet, the dome hid dangers only a strategist could see. The temptation to be everything for everybody. Only a dome built on dreams could do that.

A Dangerous Attraction

Visioning sessions play a role in your strategy process just as a vision statement plays a role in your strategic plan. A vision statement is a statement of shared aspirations, a picture of your preferred future. Your vision proclaims, "Yes, this is what we want. This will make it all worthwhile." A symbol that we all can see, much like the wonder dome.

> **Your vision is not your strategy.**

For many years, each strategic plan I wrote included a vision statement, mission statement, strategic goals, and layers of objectives, action steps, and deadlines. Everything changed when I grasped the importance of organization-level strategy: that strategy wasn't synonymous to tactic and that a brand strategy wasn't equivalent to an organizational strategy. That's when I became a strategist. That's when I understood.

> **A vision is not directional; it's aspirational.**
> **Only strategy is directional.**
> **Your direction built from a choice.**

Let that sink in for a minute. Better yet, bookmark this page and grab one or two strategic plans for purpose-driven organizations—maybe your current plan and another one. Or find a few online. When you're ready, locate the vision statements and their strategies. Any luck?

Let's take this exercise a step further. Can you tell what differentiates them in the marketplace? Did you identify their differentiators? Why they matter to their customers? Nope. That isn't clear, either. In fact, if you switched out the names of two similar organizations you may not be able to tell whose plan was whose.

As you read further, you discover something irrefutable. Their customer isn't in the plan at all. Stakeholders are there, of course. Their organization is in the spotlight. They haven't benefited from the lesson you gleaned in chapter 1. **Customer mindset guides you to discover competitive advantage.**

> **Your customer is the person whose life you promise to impact through mission delivery.**

Your Singular Advantage

"Step Three: Discover Differentiation to Drive Strategic Success" of your Four-Step Process is the signature step. It stands apart by design to delineate the act of articulating differentiation from setting strategy in "Step Four: Design Your Differentiation Zone Strategy." Here's why: this task is often given short shrift in the strategy process when, in my experience, it is the most important task of all. You can't set a differentiation strategy if you don't know what distinguishes your organization in the marketplace.

Strategists speak of competitive advantage, which is a set of attributes that position your organization to outperform competitors. You achieve what you set out to accomplish with clarity of customer, singularity of direction, and strength of purpose. You outperform on market share, financial vitality, and mission delivery.

Other strategy processes assume you understand the attributes that embody your organization's competitive advantage. Your ability to outperform competitors boils down to the essential truths, obvious and uncontested. Something that a brief conversation, some flipcharts, and a set of notes can crystallize.

Here's what this strategist has learned. You probably aren't clear about your organization's competitive advantage—and that's okay. That's why I wrote this book. You've relied on approaches that coalesce around your organization and its stakeholders. Models created before the tipping point suggest your organization defines differentiation. Aha! There's the disconnect. You are accustomed to identifying competitive advantage from your point of view, not your customer's. There is no one to say, "Really? Are you sure? That isn't special; everyone else is doing that, too." Or, even better, "I've been considering options you aren't aware of, and they have noteworthy advantages over you."

Differentiation Zone doesn't shy away from crucial conversations about competitive positioning, as we've learned with the museum. We recognize competition is inescapable. Plenty of other entities are vying for your customer's heart, mind, and wallet share due to the customer zeitgeist. Yesterday's alternative is today's replacement soon to be rivaled by something truly novel. You learned all about revealing customer insights in chapter 8.

"Step Three: Discover Differentiation to Drive Strategic Success" guides you to discover the three to five attributes that define genuine differentiation in the marketplace. Getting to that level of clarity is hard work, and other processes don't show you the way. No wonder we tether our goals to a vision and skip strategy altogether. Fortunately, your customer is here to help. **Customer mindset brings a laser focus to the attributes that position your organization to outperform competitors. Your chosen strategy converts competitive advantage into direction and results.**

Let's return to the museum. You have their play manifesto in hand, confident you understand what makes them unique. You've also left the wonder dome. Exciting as it was to visit, that bold vision can't reveal market distinction. The dome is aspirational; it isn't directional. Meet the tool that leads to your strategy destination. After you engage in a thorough overview, we'll put the tool to use.

Your Differentiation Zone Tool

As we demonstrated in chapter 2, the museum possessed untapped potential to extend the power of play to more kids and grown-ups who would benefit from it. Achieving that clarity and calling the question about it came from an understanding of customers, competitors, and context in chapters 7 and 8.

+ Zone of Indifference: **Your customer doesn't care about these features and attributes, even if you do.**

+ Competitors' Edge: **Your customer finds something unique in the offerings of your competitors.**

+ Ordinary Trap: **Your customer sees equivalence when you hope for difference.**

+ Differentiation Zone: **Your nexus. The intersection of what matters to your customer and what is truly distinctive about your organization.**

Let's tour each section of the tool.

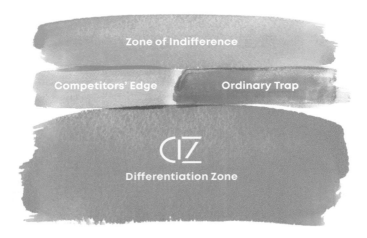

Zone of Indifference

Customer mindset reveals what doesn't matter to your customers, which you understand from "Principle Six: Avoid the Zone of Indifference." Appreciate the features and attributes that don't matter to your customer, then move them into the Zone of Indifference. They may matter to you, but your customer doesn't care about them. For example, your customer may not care about your organization's mission statement, governance structure, tax status, or proprietary software. Avoid differentiating on a feature that is in your customer's Zone of Indifference. You don't want to stake your strategy on something that doesn't matter to your customers.

Competitors' Edge

Your competitors have advantages that you do not, as we observed with Swallow Hill Music, The Logan School, and the Children's Museum. Your work in "Step Two: Reveal Customer and Competitor Insights" revealed your competitors' distinctive features and attributes. These features and benefits matter to your customer and are not part of your offering. For example, your customer may care a lot about your competitors' extended hours, inclusive programs, and ease of cancellation. Categorize them in the Competitors' Edge.

Ordinary Trap

Every product or service includes features and attributes that are ordinary, which we saw in "Step Two: Reveal Customer and Competitor Insights." These are table stakes. You need to offer these features and attributes, but they will not differentiate you in the marketplace. Likewise, you may know your feature is different from your competitors, but your customer may believe they are equivalent. Guess what? That doesn't matter. If your customer feels they are the same, then they are. Your customer may not fully understand the distinctions, may not care, or may be confused. We've named this a trap because you don't want to build your strategy around the ordinary. That's a sure path to organizational decline.

Group the ordinary elements together and place them here. Relying on them as differentiators is a sure path to diminished market share when your competitors have unique attributes that you do not possess.

Differentiation Zone

We've been working our way down a funnel, of sorts, in search of your organization's true differentiators. You set aside the attributes that don't matter, you looked at where your competitors have an edge, and you admitted that you might feel proud of a feature or two that are ordinary in your industry. You've recognized the attributes that won't position you to outperform competitors.

Now you have a clear view of the shortlist of attributes that shine through. These attributes matter to your customers. And, better yet, they are solely yours. Say hello to your Differentiation Zone, home to the extraordinary, special, and one-of-a-kind attributes that matter most to your customer.

Declaring Differentiation

You are ready to complete the Differentiation Zone Tool for your organization. Bring the strategic insights gleaned from "Step Two: Reveal Customer and

Competitor Insights" as you prepare for an iterative decision-making process. Your goal is to coalesce around a shortlist of attributes and features that collectively describe your organization's uniqueness.

Remember to be the customer as you facilitate this activity. When you think of your customer in third person, pivot to place them in first-person. It requires a bit of practice, but once you get the hang of it, the insights flow.

When I facilitate these conversations, I use statements and questions to test underlying assumptions and push for consensus-based clarity. That technique also helps me retain a customer mindset. Here's an example of the types of statements and questions you may use to group the attributes and features from your analysis from "Step Two: Reveal Customer and Competitor Insights" to your tool's four sections. Note your customer is in the first-person point of view.

+ Customers don't care about X feature. Let's place X in the Zone of Indifference.
  • For example, the museum's customers may be indifferent to their affiliation with an international trade association.
+ Customers believe A, B, and C attributes are unique to competitors. Do competitors have an edge according to our customers? If so, let's place those features in the Competitors' Edge.
  • For example, the museum's competitors may offer wonderful home-based experiences that rival the in-person visit.
+ Customers consider features B and C to be ordinary. They can't tell us apart from the competition. Those features go in the Ordinary Trap.
  • For example, the organizations may offer similar membership perks.

Envision your group scanning the visuals created in "Step Two: Reveal Customer and Competitor Insights" as you lead a real-time analysis of each feature and attribute.

Reveal What Matters
Most to Your Customers

 Shrugs (these don't matter)	Smiles (these matter; and some matter a lot)

Reveal Uniqueness
in the Marketplace

Unique to Competitors:

_____

Not Unique to Any Organization:

_____

Unique to Your Organization:

_____

Iteration leads to a stronger process and is essential to discover insights. I've found it beneficial to facilitate this conversation during two meetings, allowing time to process and affirm your decisions. Your conversation will cycle back and forth as you sift and sort through the features and attributes, calling the question as you go. That's to be expected. In fact, I'd worry if you didn't question, challenge, and double-check a few times. You want to evoke emotional reactions, too, linking head and heart. As your team engages in these thought-provoking conversations, don't get stuck in your heads. Lead with your hearts. Imagine you are the customer. Feel what matters most to them. Scan the options from their point of view, then step back to unveil the destination.

Your differentiators live at the intersection between why your organization matters and what makes your organization unique. I refer to that point as the nexus. This is your Differentiation Zone.

The Nexus: Your Differentiators

Give yourselves time to acclimate to your discovery. Look back at your Differentiation Zone tool and what you've grouped under each of the four categories. Call the question one more time to ensure your Differentiation Zone includes a combination of three to five genuine and compelling concepts. Do you feel that visceral sense of achievement I mentioned earlier? Are you sitting up and taking notice? Is it exciting and affirming? Aha! Those words and phrases are the basis of your differentiation strategy. If not, iterate one more time. You'll know when you've arrived.

Learning Moment

Before we continue with the museum's differentiation process, let's pause to connect this learning moment with the book's introduction and The Logan School's story. When you met me in the school's lunchroom, you observed me embrace a customer mindset for The Logan School, in which I:

+ Understood what mattered most to gifted students
+ Realized what was unique to Logan

That nexus, like the marker on a map, signified the destination. A unique intersection that only Logan could claim. The school had proven that these kids could drive their education from a young age. Creative thinking affirmed the realization. The school was clearly differentiated. We discovered Logan's Differentiation Zone.

You can't skip "Step Three: Discover Differentiation to Drive Strategic Success," or give it short shrift, without consequence. What do you risk? A false sense of differentiation based on stakeholder hope rather than customer insight grounded in marketplace realities. That will likely land you in the Ordinary Trap—or worse, the Zone of Indifference. The Children's Museum might have found itself there if it didn't have the courage to embrace what mattered most to its customers—the kids—and caregivers considering myriad options in the customer zeitgeist.

Let's return to the museum to welcome its discovery.

Discovering the Zone

Wonder freed the Children's Museum of Denver at Marsico Campus to envision what could be. Customer mindset grounded museum leaders in what needed to be. I was thrilled to see it come together. The museum's differentiator was revealed. I'd learned so much through our experience with The Logan School. I knew what an authentic insight felt like, the visceral reaction of someone sitting up and taking notice. The head-heart realization that this is true, genuine, and unique.

We found the museum's Differentiation Zone.

+ What mattered most to the museum's customers?
+ What was unique about the museum?

Let's apply the same design element to the Children's Museum that we did with The Logan School to solidify your learning. Feel free to refer back to Logan's visual to spark your own "aha" moment.

That nexus, like the marker on a map, signified the destination. This was a unique intersection that only they could claim. Iterative thinking and testing of insights affirmed the conclusion.

 Everything that mattered most to the museum's customers, from cool stuff for kids of all ages to adult-friendly offerings and multicultural inclusion, is embraced in its 2030 Master Plan. The museum was clearly differentiated. We discovered the museum's Differentiation Zone.

The Children's Museum of Denver at Marsico Campus gives people of all ages permission to play.

The power of play will be accessible to all at the Children's Museum of Denver at Marsico Campus. A customer mindset made sure of it.

Your Customer Reveals the Answers You Seek

Your customer's answers lead you to declare your organization's differentiators, which is a critical milestone en route to creating your differentiation strategy. Our learnings with the museum illustrate the iterative nature of discovery. Original insights illuminate authentic distinction in the marketplace. The museum's leaders were brave, too, willing to stand in grace as they explored areas of excellence and heard customer desires for more.

Your customer enlightens your thinking about competitive advantage and differentiation throughout this step of your process. It's as if your customer is in the room with you calling the question and challenging you to look deeper, feel what they feel, delineate more clearly, and not take anything for granted. Customer mindset asks you to push for honesty as you shine a laser-focused light on what matters most. You do it because you are committed to your customers. Your mission makes that promise.

"Step Three: Discover Differentiation to Drive Strategic Success" of your Four-Step Process encapsulates everything we've learned together so far. Grab your highlighter as you look back.

> What does customer mindset mean for strategy?
> Everything. What matters most to your
> customer matters most to you. Differentiation
> is determined by your customer.

I'll ask you to stay in a place of grace and courage. Your organization has important choices to make in chapter 10. Next up, strategy.

10.

Step Four: Design Your Differentiation Zone Strategy

Seeing Beyond What Is

We debated about terminology during our quest to brand the strategic plan for the College of Arts, Humanities & Social Sciences at the University of Denver. We wanted to symbolize the entirety of the plan—its vision, strategy, and call to action.

What role did a liberal and creative arts education play in the undergraduate experience? Was it the cornerstone, the keystone, or the foundation? The keystone is the central piece at the top of the arch, tying it all together. Creativity and critical thought, originality and rigor, liberal and creative arts—the college tied the undergraduate experience together. The dean understood the totality of their mission relevance.

After months of meetings, furrowed brows, iterative thinking, and standing resolute, the plan was coming together. We'd sifted and sorted through everything we'd heard—the ideas, aspirations, must-dos, unyielding competitive pressures, and evolving customer expectations. Change was inescapable. The college would answer the call.

Who knew at the start that we'd end up with a commitment to reimagining a liberal and creative arts education? When I first met the dean and heard about the college's in-process strategic plan, I was struck by the limitations of its SWOT. After reading through the analysis and reflecting on my work with the engineering school mentioned in chapter 7, I understood what we needed to do. The Internet of Things was coming and so was a generation of undergraduates who demanded more. I pushed the dean and faculty to see beyond what is.

Customer Mindset Is the Keystone

Customer mindset revealed that students expected a holistic education filled with robust academics and creative collaboration. They craved real-world opportunities to apply their learning across the liberal and creative arts, just as you observed with the prospective student in chapter 7. The college also anticipated the forces influencing competitor moves. We referred to them as gale-force winds during our discussion of context in chapter 4. Competitors were certain to find their own edge in the marketplace. Yet they didn't possess the college's unique set of differentiators.

> Your customer is the person whose life you promise to impact through mission delivery.

No other college committed to innovation to this degree or in this way. Other campuses didn't encompass the full spectrum of the liberal and creative arts under one roof. The untapped synergies and collaborative potential across the college were assets the dean was eager to maximize in the college's new strategy.

Creativity and innovation were oft-used words across campus and in higher education. Science, technology, engineering, and math (STEM) and business frequently used both terms. The chosen strategy couldn't convey mere lip service to the expected. We couldn't afford to create a plan that looked like every other college's plan. Future success depended on authentic commitment and bold, quick action. There was no time to waste. Transformation was our mantra.

The newly designed Keystone Experience would differentiate the college in the marketplace through its integrated, immersive, and multifaceted educational experience. Students could create custom learning experiences, encompassing the liberal and creative arts and beyond. For example, the prospective student we met in chapter 7 could bust the boundaries between STEM, the arts, humanities, and social sciences. Anything an undergraduate imagined could be realized in partnership with faculty devoted to advancing new knowledge with real-world application.

Faculty innovation was the turbocharge necessary to accelerate strategic success. In a few short years, the plan affirmed the college's mission and strategic relevance. An innovation center provided a setting for the first publicly staged theater production whose actors were prisoners. The play, produced on a downtown stage in Denver, would be the first time that prisoners acted in public in the United States. Faculty didn't need a push to do that; they'd wanted to do it all along. The college recognized what mattered most to students and what made it unique in the marketplace.

Their spotlight had shifted, and the customer was center stage. The college would reinvent liberal and creative arts through boundary-spanning educational experiences and a faculty innovation center.

Relevance Is Forward Looking

How did the college convert its differentiators into a successful differentiation strategy? Let's remind ourselves of a few strategy fundamentals. Strategy sets your organization's course of action for the timeframe selected, whether that's two, three, five, or ten years. Your charge? Leverage your differentiators to fill an opening in the marketplace that matters to customers and positions you to outperform competitors. Look for a marketplace opening that is strategic rather than opportunistic. You know something is opportunistic if it only takes advantage of immediate circumstances. Rest assured, you don't want to base your strategy on chance or the whim of occasion.

"Step Four: Design Your Differentiation Zone Strategy" applies everything we've learned so far. All of the Six Guiding Principles come into play as you set strategy. "Principle One: It's All About the Customer" sets the foundation when it announced the customer mindset's essential role in achieving mission and strategic relevance. Relevance is future focused. Your organization's significance is framed by the Three Cs—customers, competitors, and context—as explored in section 1. The Zone of Indifference screams of irrelevance, doesn't it? Your organization won't matter much in three years if you've built your strategy on the unimportant. Remember, it's not about what your stakeholders think. Your customer's choice directs the action.

Pull out your highlighter again as you recall learnings from chapters 7 and 9. The Three Cs came together in "Step One: Understand Your Customers, Competitors, and Context," placing your differentiators in context. You learned to be the customer. That analysis showed you how to focus on the forces with the greatest potential to shape or drive your future strategy. Study the three to five forces with the power to drive customer choices over your plan's time horizon, noting which will likely influence competitor actions.

Customer and competitor insights from "Step Two: Reveal Customer and Competitor Insights" were the starting point for "Step Three: Discover Differentiation to Drive Strategic Success," revealing your organization's competitive positioning. You articulated your Differentiation Zone, taking note of your Competitors' Edge while avoiding the Ordinary Trap and Zone of Indifference.

Now your task is to anticipate openings in the marketplace that maximize your Differentiation Zone, just as the dean did. Spot the gaps your organization can uniquely fill, taking advantage of the forces that align with your differentiators. Most importantly, look for the forces with the potential to accelerate differentiation, just like the college did. Your competitors don't have an edge here, and your customer cares a lot. Conversely, keep an eye out for the forces influencing competitor actions that support or reinforce their Competitors' Edge, which will likely have a continued advantage over your organization. Now you've parlayed your differentiators into a Differentiation Zone strategy. Name and claim your future direction in a statement or two.

Relevance is the foundation of strategic differentiation. If you don't understand what makes your organization unique and distinctive in the marketplace, your strategy won't achieve its intended results. And then, what's the point? You may as well tether your goals to a vision. Customer mindset ensures you don't get trapped into thinking that you and your stakeholders determine relevance. That's up to your customer. Your customer's voice is the clarion call when crafting your mission and setting your strategy.

The Stage Is Set

Customer mindset tied it all together for the college, just as it will for you. As you open your mind to the power of customer mindset, you'll find your stage more distinctive, exciting, and compelling.

The first three steps armed you with everything you need to know about your customers, competitors, and context. Now you are poised to create your competition-proof strategy using the differentiators you declared in "Step Three: Discover Differentiation to Drive Strategic Success." You'll build a plan, make your strategy a reality, and, if desired, optimize your business model. The college and its Keystone Strategic Plan is a case study for both. You know its strategy by now. Its innovation center is an example of business model optimization in higher education.

Step One: Understand Your Customers, Competitors, and Context.
Step Two: Reveal Customer and Competitor Insights.
Step Three: Discover Differentiation to Drive Strategic Success.
Step Four: Design Your Differentiation Zone Strategy.

If the essence of your strategy is choice, then the foundation of differentiation strategy is customer mindset. Not only do you need to get it, but so does your team—your board, faculty, management, and staff. Approachable and relatable, each step encourages your board and staff to bring their experiences to the process of setting strategy. Together you:

+ Clarify your customer and honor your stakeholder.
+ Address competition from unexpected places.
+ Focus on the external forces with the power to shape your organization's future.
+ Say, "Yes, that goes in the Zone of Indifference."

Everyone learns together, sharing discoveries and new ideas. Together, you build common understanding and shared meaning, which results in a clear strategy that can be embraced with agility, as we have seen with the Keystone Strategic Plan. Rather than end in fatigue, the final step of your process is an exciting affirmation of what makes your organization distinctive. No longer the best-kept secret, your organization is positioned to accelerate success.

Principle One: It's All About the Customer.

Principle Two: Not Every Stakeholder Is a Customer.

Principle Three: Competition Is Prevalent.

Principle Four: Your Environment Creates Context, Not Focus.

Principle Five: You Compete in More Than One Industry.

Principle Six: Watch Out for the Zone of Indifference.

The Essence of Your Strategy Is Choice

Today's strategic plan has a big job. A plan's success rests in its ability to capture the imagination, inspire others, and convert inspiration into action in the form of new partnerships and expanded funding. You won't achieve results of that magnitude with a simple set of goals and to-do lists. Your strategic plan must sell, on its own, to an external audience of deciders, influencers, stakeholders, and customers. Why do you matter? Why should you matter to me? In my experience, the most successful strategic plans engage the reader in the story of why you matter and your plan to accelerate mission impact.

The dean and I realized the college needed to reassert the importance of a liberal and creative arts education to the university and to society. The difference between a keystone and a cornerstone is subtle, yet significant. We asked the important question, "Are we part of the foundation or the center connecting everything together?" The metaphor symbolized the plan's call to action in a mere three pages. Then, pow! The analogy illustrates the significance of the vision and strategic priorities.

The process of claiming the college's centrality to the university's mission in this disruptive era gave the dean and faculty courage to step out in a bold way. Their proclamation was audacious. The Keystone Strategic Plan became a unifying voice for everyone within the college and a means for standing out among a growing array of competitors. They committed to invest in the active cultivation of invention, discovery, imagination, creativity, teaching, and learning.

Differentiation Zone leads you to a singular strategy distinctive from other organizations. The true measures of an effective strategy are the results achieved and your plan's ability to motivate, inspire, and activate. The mission was fulfilled in service to customers and community.

I've long believed that an exciting plan inspires someone to make a donation. That's often the biggest compliment a plan can receive. Others deem it worthy of investment. Six- and seven-figure gifts affirmed the college's choice of strategy. Higher education is an exceptionally competitive market for fundraising. Attracting gifts of that magnitude from highly discerning investors meant that they'd realized the powerful through line I referenced in the introduction. Let's highlight it again now.

> A differentiation strategy driven by customer mindset elevates your customer to the organization level, allowing you to craft a strategy with a powerful through line to mission-relevant success measures.

The Keystone Strategic Plan embodied the college's hero's journey, as did the 2030 Master Plan for the Children's Museum of Denver at Marsico Campus. The museum's search for differentiation took it to the moon and back. Your journey to differentiation is guided by an imperative. You have to say no to say yes. The college's strategy was declared. Ordinary wouldn't do.

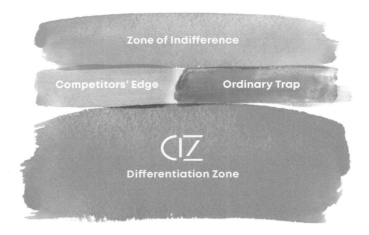

A Singular Sense of Direction

At long last your Differentiation Zone process is complete. Your purpose-driven organization is powerfully differentiated. Your strategic plan is the compelling story of your organization's definitive yes.

11.

Your Strategy Declaration

Your Studio Awaits

When I discovered The Logan School's Differentiation Zone, I didn't envision creating a new approach to strategy. One realization led to another, cascading into uncharted territory. Iterative thinking and real-time learning served to reinforce, test, revamp, and improve. Along the way, my commitment to the power of customer mindset strengthened. So did my belief in your essential differentiators. My strategy declaration was firmly in hand.

Now I see how ripe the strategy field is for creativity. The tipping point is pushing us to think beyond what is and leave the old frameworks behind.

We've been trained to believe we are in the strategy spotlight as leaders, consultants, stakeholders, and organizations; that what we think and what we do matters most. I'm asking you to unwind all that and start anew. Years of strategic planning, decades of SWOT, and the belief that all stakeholders are customers prevent you from embracing differentiation from a customer mindset.

I'm inviting you to make your strategy declaration.

If your purpose-driven organization is pursuing a cost strategy, by all means, do so with gusto. Do so with aplomb. Own it. And let me know how it goes. I'd love to learn alongside you.

If your purpose-driven organization isn't pursuing a cost strategy, then know you are, by default, pursuing a differentiation strategy whether or not you realize it. Rest assured that you don't want an ordinary strategic plan or a strategy based in the easily mimicked because you were swept up by stakeholder sentiment or the belief that you don't really have competitors. If you are, prepare to be met with confusion when a discerning reader can't tell your plan apart from your competitor's. It happens more often than you realize. A pleasant smile and nod mask the underlying truth. Your customer and stakeholder don't understand what makes you special or one of a kind. They aren't clear about your strategic direction because you don't really have one. Alas, your plan is nothing more than a set of goals tethered to a vision.

> Your customer is the person whose life you promise to impact through mission delivery.

My hope is that you have the opportunity, as I did with The Logan School, to receive heartfelt applause for achieving authentic insights about what matters most. My career has never been the same. Differentiation Zone is my gift to you in honor of every organization that has trusted me with their strategy.

As you prepare your strategy declaration, I'll remind you of mine. Differentiation is determined by your customer.

Your Path to Discovery

Creative thinking is embedded throughout Differentiation Zone. A co-created process of ideation and iteration reveals true differentiation in the marketplace. At the core are context, connections, and insights. Your process prompts critical conversations about competitive advantage and examines the environmental factors that affect your customers' actions. Through iterative conversations with ever-widening circles of stakeholders, influencers, and deciders, your organization's opportunity to reinvent itself evolves and solidifies. As new ideas resonate, the audacious notions gain momentum and become your mantra. Be the customer.

Differentiation Zone is flexible. Not only can you use it to facilitate a strategy process for your purpose-driven organization, but you can also solidify differentiation of your brand, fundraising, alumni program, and other supporting strategies. You can use the first three steps of the process to analyze current strategic positioning, or you can engage in the entire Four-Step Process to craft a differentiation strategy and plan for your organization.

Step One: Understand Your Customers, Competitors, and Context.
Step Two: Reveal Customer and Competitor Insights.
Step Three: Discover Differentiation to Drive Strategic Success.
Step Four: Design Your Differentiation Zone Strategy.

+ The first three steps lead you to define strategic differentiation in the marketplace for your organization, brand, or fundraising effort. Your differentiators are all you need to advance your branding, marketing, or fundraising efforts. The same is true if you want to craft a differentiation strategy for alumni engagement or membership.
+ Add the fourth step to the first three to create your differentiation strategy and plan. Both aid you in revising your business model for optimal alignment with your new strategy.

Discover Your Strategy Community

A friend remarked that synthesis is my superpower. Differentiation Zone and its full suite of digital resources bring together everything I've discovered to advance your success. If you are committed to differentiation from a customer mindset, please know I am here for you. You'll have ready access to tools, coaching, case studies, consulting, and a community of strategists with a shared passion to advance their craft and the purpose-driven organizations that matter to them. Welcome to your digital strategy experience.

Final Word

There's never been a more important time to stand out in the marketplace. Unexpected competitor moves, blurring industry boundaries, and disinterest in tax status propel you to envision a bold future for your organization. Some of your industries are in the midst of radical reinvention; the pandemic's distortion powers are unrivaled.

Differentiation is essential. So, too, is a clear strategy.

I hope I've inspired you to push beyond what you think is possible. To claim the rightful place for your customer at the center of your strategy process and the heart of your strategic plan.

You are ready to facilitate a Differentiation Zone process for an organization that means the world to you. Your studio awaits. I look forward to seeing your creation.

Acknowledgements

I am incredibly grateful to so many people. This book represents decades of learning, growth, opportunity, "aha" moments, and partnership with tremendous people and purpose-driven organizations that believed in my work and valued my contributions, most notably to my consulting clients who have trusted me with their strategy. This book is for you.

To my Differentiation Zone team, past and present, you are the wind beneath my wings. Most notably, to Denise for saying during the early days of the pandemic, "Karla, this may be the time to write your book." I was ready to meet the moment. Thank you for suggesting it. Your steadfast belief in my bold idea has sustained me.

Rebecca, without your encouragement at just the right moments, this book wouldn't be what it is today. Thank you for serving as my first reader. You are a gift. To my colleagues who read, commented, and encouraged me, thank you.

To my Corona Insights colleagues present and past, your contributions to our strategy clients and Differentiation Zone's many moving parts are greatly appreciated. You were there for Logan's eureka moment and had the wisdom to spot what became the Zone of Indifference. I'm grateful for it all.

I am blessed with friends who love me for my total self, particularly Sandy and James. Thank you for your friendship.

To my brother, Mark, with love. Differentiation Zone sprung to life as we honored our parents and their legacy.

To my parents, Carl and Phyllis—the Viking and the artist—for embodying courage and creativity. I've channeled you many times during the writing of this book. Everything I inherited from you lives on here. This is your legacy coming to life through me.

To Kevin, through thick or thin, whatever is better. You are the love of my life.

About the Author

Karla Raines didn't pick up a paintbrush until 2012, although she's been creating works of art for her clients in the form of compelling strategic plans for more than twenty years. Effortlessly moving disparate elements into a curated and cohesive whole, Karla provides purpose-driven organizations with sought-after clarity and focus.

As principal and co-owner of Corona Insights, a highly regarded research and strategy firm based in Denver, Karla has helped hundreds of organizations craft their strategic plans. Along the way, she devoted more than ten thousand hours to mastering the art of strategy. A skilled associative thinker, Karla uses her intuition and both sides of her brain to make cognitive leaps. She sees new opportunities in a shifting strategic landscape and conveys them in ways that build buy-in and excitement for her clients.

Comfort with ambiguity is critical to her success as a strategist and as an abstract artist. Karla engages more boldly as a consultant because of her artistic endeavors. She believes that "creating art requires a high tolerance for risk because you never know if the next stroke is going to enhance or diminish the work. You learn to give yourself permission to make mistakes." And her risk-taking is one of the qualities clients appreciate most. "Karla gave board members the confidence and courage to take a stand," remarked one of her clients.

"Strategy is all about choice," says Karla. You have to say yes to some options and, equally importantly, no to others. Being an artist requires the same discipline. "You learn to let go of a piece that holds great attachment for you yet falls short artistically. Let's face it—some stuff simply isn't good. Do it anyway. Love it. Share it with the world. Then let it go," she adds.

Karla earned her MBA from The University of Texas at Austin McCombs School of Business and her BS in industrial engineering from Iowa State University. She and her husband, Kevin, live in Denver.

CPSIA information can be obtained
at www.ICGtesting.com
Printed in the USA
BVHW021806250121
598383BV00004B/4/J

9 781736 477007